Histories from the Cotswold Edge

Histories *from the* Cotswold Edge

DAVID H ALDRED

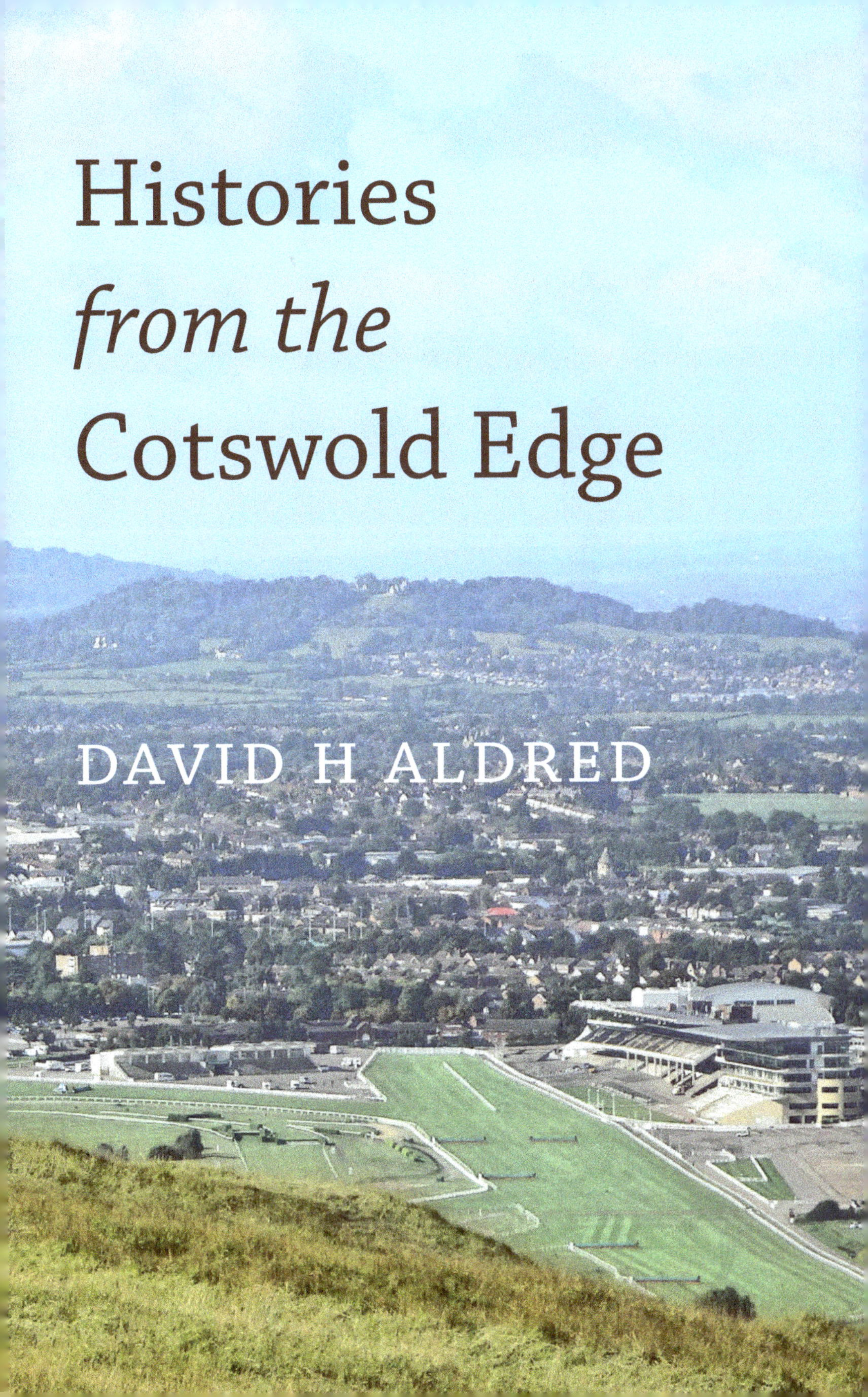

First published in the United Kingdom in 2025
by The Hobnob Press,
8 Lock Warehouse, Severn Road, Gloucester GL1 2GA
www.hobnobpress.co.uk

British Library Cataloguing in Publication Data
A catalogue record for this book is available from the British Library

ISBN 978-1-914407-99-4

Typeset in Chaparral Pro, 11/14 pt
Typesetting and origination by John Chandler

CONTENTS

THE
Bishop's Cleeve,
Woodmancote
and now also *Winchcombe*
DIRECTORY

ISSUE 4
FREE

YOUR INDEPENDENT
COMMUNITY MAGAZINE

JUNE/JULY 2010   www.thebishopscleevedirectory.co.uk

WORLD CUP
Fixtures list inside!

Gardening
Scented Pelargoniums

Technology Review
Happy Snaps

Recipe
Strawberry & Cream Cake

Pubs & Restaurants listings
Useful Local Information inside

WIN
Theatre Tickets
The Everyman Theatre
Prescott Speed-Hill Climb Tickets
Midland Championships

**Children's Page
and so much more!**

PREFACE

THIS IS A BOOK for dipping into. In its pages you can read new insights into the well-known histories of Cheltenham races and the Honeybourne railway line to the little-known visit of Queen Elizabeth I's visit to Sudeley Castle and the fascinating story of the Guiting Power Stone Pipe Works. These wide-ranging articles first appeared in a local history series I wrote for the *Directory* - a free monthly advertising magazine which appeared in Bishop's Cleeve in December 2009, soon to be expand into Winchcombe, then Cheltenham, Prestbury, and as far as Tewkesbury and even Newent. The *Directory* ceased publication in 2020 during the covid epidemic and my last article appeared in January of that year. During that decade many people approached me to ask if I could gather the articles together into a permanent volume. So this is it, nearly six years on from my last article.

However, this is not just a re-publication of the original articles as I am fully aware that changes have taken place since they appeared and so I have revisited and updated those articles I have selected from my original sixty two. I have merged some into a longer account than the original double-page page spread, particularly where I kept a contemporary theme going across the years, for examples the articles I wrote each year at the time of the Gold Cup with their horse-racing theme or those which reflected the centenary commemorations of the First World War. So even if you kept the original articles, you'll find much more of interest here. To give some coherence to my choice of articles the focus is the Cotswold edge with the adjoining vale, principally from Cheltenham in the south to Winchcombe and Broadway in the north with a handful covering Cotswold villages to the east wherever I found there was an interesting story to tell. The photographs and other illustrations are a mixture of original and more recent, depending upon the subject content. They were taken by me or are from my collection. Where this is not so, I have acknowledged the sources in the caption.

Neither the original articles or those in this volume could have been written without the assistance of many people to whom I am grateful. First and foremost my thanks go to Vicky Muller and Anne Golldack of the *Directory* for inviting me to write the original articles. My thanks also go to the following for their help in compiling this volume: Charlie Aldred, Michael Bates, Anne Crow, Ian Crowder, the late Tim Curr, Simon Draper, Stephanie Duensing, Christopher Dyer, Mike Edwards, David Gray, Derek Maddock, Caroline Mellor, Andy Moir, Ruth Owen-Overton, John Reid, Alastair Robinson, Phil Robson, Peter Weale, Susanne Weir. The staff at Gloucestershire Archives and Bishop's Cleeve and Cheltenham libraries have been unfailingly helpful. My thanks also go to John Chandler and Louise Ryland-Epton of Hobnob Press for their support in the publishing of the book. My greatest thanks go to my wife Margaret for all the support she has given me over the decade during which I wrote the articles and more recently for commenting upon the drafts of this book. Any shortcomings of course remain my own.

David Aldred
November 2025

PLACE NAMES

What's in a Name?

I wrote my very first article for the Bishop's Cleeve directory in 2010. In it I attempted to explain the meaning of some of the local place names. Place names are important as they can give clues to how people viewed their landscapes in the past. The key to understanding them is not to guess from today's names but to investigate the earliest recording of the name and notice the earliest spelling. However we must always keep in mind the settlement is more likely to have been older than the first appearance of its name in the written record.

I continued a study of place names with three more articles, starting with Winchcombe and area, then moving to the north Cotswolds and ending in Cheltenham. I have combined the four articles into this single account.

THE EARLIEST KNOWN recording of the name of Bishop's Cleeve can be found in a document dated 777–779AD. 'Cleeve' means 'at the cliff'; the cliff of course refers to Cleeve Hill. Within a century the area came into the hands of the Bishop of Worcester and 'Bishop's' (with

Bishop's Cleeve lies below the hill from which it took its name

The medieval meadow of Muckmead after which Southam might have been named is two thirds of the ploughed feature

an apostrophe!) was added to distinguish it from Cleeve Prior which lies on the banks of the River Avon north of Evesham. This belonged to Worcester Priory, the community of monks living at Worcester Cathedral. The earliest recording of 'Bishop's' was in a document dated 1284. So what might other local names mean?

Southam is the earliest recorded, about 991. It comprises two elements, 'South' refers to its position south of Bishop's Cleeve, but historians still debate the meaning of 'ham'. It could mean a homestead or small settlement but it could also mean a water meadow (i.e. a meadow for growing hay which was flooded with water in the spring to encourage the grass to grow). Evidence to support the latter theory is provided by an area called Northenham i.e. the north water meadow, now covered in the houses of Cleeve Gardens bordering the A435 to the north of the village centre.

Southam was recorded in Domesday Book of 1086 in an entry which also included Gotherington and a settlement which has completely disappeared called *Sapletone*. Gotherington means the settlement associated with a man called Guthere. Later references indicate this was a small settlement lying below the manor house on the lower slopes of Nottingham Hill at the end of Manor Lane. *Sapletone* was first recorded in 969 as *Saperetun*, the settlement or homestead of the soap makers. It was last recorded in 1300 and probably lay somewhere between Southam and Stoke Orchard.

Also recorded in Domesday Book was Stoke. It means a small settlement dependent upon another; in this case Tewkesbury. We can use Stoke Orchard as an example of the need to be vigilant in explaining place names. In 1208 John Archer held it from the king by providing an archer when needed for the army, thus Stoke Archer. The Archer family died out about 1350 and as people forgot the meaning of the original name it was rationalised to Stoke Orchard.

The name 'Orchard' estate in Stoke Orchard can mislead people into thinking that this was the original orchard after which the village was named. The bishop's valley runs diagonally across the centre of this view (below), which also shows some of the surviving woodland above Woodmancote

Woodmancote was not recorded until about 1200 but its meaning is obvious – the woodman's cottage or shed, no doubt linked to the extensive woodland on the slopes of Nottingham Hill and Cleeve Hill. The bishop's valley i.e. Bushcombe, was first recorded in 1299. It lies between Cleeve Hill and Nottingham Hill, which was named after the Bishop of Worcester's steward William Nottingham between1460 and 1470. This replaced the earlier name for the hill which survives today as Cockbury, first recorded in the early 11th century as *Coccanburh*, the name given to the Iron Age camp on top of the hill. *Cocca* was either a personal name or a mythical name – nobody today is quite sure.

Winchcombe in its valley

The earliest record of Winchcombe so far discovered is *Wincelcumba* dating from about 800AD. It means a corner or bend (*wincel*) in a valley (*cumb*). *Cumb* was used to describe a short valley surrounded by three hills with a dead end. Today cyclists struggling up Cleeve Hill along the B4632 might appreciate the accuracy of the description. Interestingly Winchcombe is unique in being the only historical town situated in a *cumb* valley in England. Should there be an 'e' at the end? Until the late 1800s it was more common to omit the 'e' but since then it has normally been used. The next time you visit Cheltenham, take a look at the old spelling on the nineteenth-century street sign on the corner of High Street and Winchcombe Street.

Winchcombe without the 'e'

Winchcombe street names are first recorded much later and most are straightforward to understand: North Street (1184), High Street (1217), Vineyard Street (1270). An interesting exception is Cowl Lane, with the earliest recording as *Colestrete* in 1269. The name has nothing to do with cows or the cowls worn by the monks at the abbey, but refers to charcoal. Whether charcoal was made there, bought and sold there or stored there will probably always remain a mystery.

The town's agricultural past is commemorated by 'Enfield', found along Back Lane, first recorded in 1539 and meaning the infield: that part of the common fields closest to the town and therefore cultivated every year. Beyond the infield lies Langley, first recorded in 1462, and referring to 'a/the long clearing' made when the hill was largely covered

by trees. On the opposite side of the Isbourne valley, Corndean (1181) has been interpreted as a valley with a corn mill, although the nearest are along the River Isbourne at the bottom of the valley and so another interpretation might be 'a valley where cranes live'.

There is still extensive woodland above Sudeley Castle

Dean comes from *denu* which means a long narrow valley which slopes gently, with moderately steep sides. Isbourne was first recorded in Worcestershire in 709AD, meaning 'the stream of *Esa's* people'. It flows into the River Avon at Evesham.

The earliest record of Sudeley is *Sudlege* in Domesday Book and then as *Suthleia* in 1175. This seems to mean 'a/the clearing to the south (of Winchcombe)'. However, it has also been argued that such a meaning would have produced the name Southley and that the present name really means 'a/the clearing with a shed', although whose shed and for what

Local names on a signpost. Prescot (sic) means 'the priest's cottage'. In 1175 Winchcombe Abbey had a chapel there

purpose have been lost in the mists of time. Beyond Sudeley, Spoonley (1287) means 'a/the clearing where wood chippings were left'. This indicates a place where wooden tiles, or shingles, were made for use on the roofs of buildings in Winchcombe. It is yet another 'ley' name indicating the extensive woodlands which once surrounded the town.

Finally, we can move to the vale. Greet was first recorded as *Greta* in 1185 and means 'a/the gravelly place'. *Grettun* was also first recorded in 1185. Its obvious meaning is 'the farmstead on the gravel' but this causes problems for the experts as there is no obvious area of gravel in the village. As a result it has been suggested Gretton means the farmstead near Greet. More research needs to be done here.

After articles on Bishop's Cleeve and Winchcombe areas, I turned to the place names of a wider area.

I started with Alderton. The name might suggest a farmstead or settlement ('ton') where alder trees grew. However, the earliest name, recorded in 1059, was *Aldritone*. Experts believe that the name was originally in three parts, meaning the farmstead or settlement (tone) of the people connected with (i) a man called *Ealdhere* (Aldr). The same format can be applied to nearby Toddington (*Tuda*) and Teddington

Alderton

Stow was first recorded about 1107 as St Edward's Stow i.e. church. Since writing the original article in October 2013, this signpost is now a protected ancient monument

(*Teotta*). But the interest in these three names does not end here. Toddington's earliest written record is found in Domesday Book in 1086;

Teddington's appeared in 780AD. The similarity in the type of name suggests that Alderton and Toddington are also likely to have been formed by 780AD, and in all probability all three names were in existence a century or so before then. Teddington has a further mystery, for the name *Teotta* has never been found anywhere else, except in Tettenhall in Staffordshire. It's just possible that it was a pet name for Theobald, who gave his name to the Tibblestone which still stands at Teddington Hands and which was first recorded in Domesday Book.

From the vale if we travel along the B4277 up Stanway Hill we reach

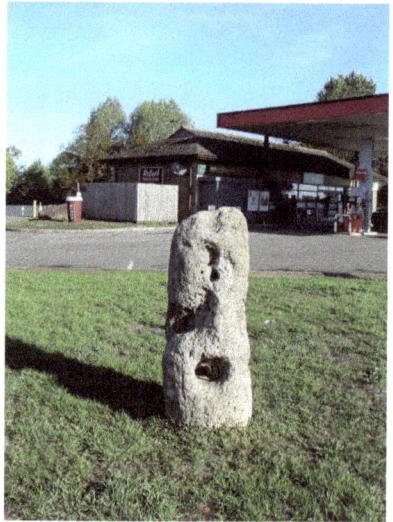

The Tibblestone at Teddington Hands. It was erected here only in 1948; its original position is not known

Ford where the road crosses the infant River Windrush. The meaning of the name here is obvious and it has remained the same since its earliest recording in 1154. Then, by following the river upstream, we reach Cutsdean where the name has far more intrigue. Cutsdean appears to mean 'Cod's *denu*' - Cod being a male personal name. However the earliest recorded spelling is *Codestun* in 977 i.e. Cod's homestead or village. Over time 'tun' became 'dean'. By 1221 the 'd' had been replaced by 't' in some spellings. The name 'Cod' was found in other names in the immediate area, *Codswell* in 780AD and *Codsbury* in 1055. This has even led scholars to think that 'Cotswold' was first applied to this area of the north Cotswolds before it was applied to the wider area we know today.

Cutsdean

The earliest recording of 'Cotswold' is somewhat later than these place names, appearing first in the 1100s. It is likely to have meant Cod's *wald*, a wooded area of high ground. Only after 1200 did it come to mean just the high ground – the wold, after the trees had been cut down. Experts still discuss the origin of the name 'Cotswold' but next time you read or hear that it signifies a wold with sheep cots, think 'codswallop' by remembering the advice to explore the meaning of a place name from its earliest form.

The River Windrush near Temple Guiting flowing gently

On the Cotswolds we find the landscape itself is more likely to provide the distinguishing features, rather than people. Many readers will have visited Bourton on the Water where the River Windrush makes the centre of the village so attractive. Few, if any, might realise the earliest name for the river was the Guiting brook (*Gythingebroc*) first recorded in 780AD and meaning 'a torrent or fast-flowing river'. Upstream from Bourton the river gave its name to a large area of land. About 1160 some of the land was given to the Knights Templar – a religious society which had been set up to encourage soldiers to fight in the Crusades in the Holy Land. So Temple Guiting gained its name, to distinguish it from the settlement a little further south near the same river. This has been known in the past as Lower or Nether Guiting but we know it today as Guiting Power. This was first recorded in 1220 when

Guiting Power

it was in the hands of le Poher family (hence 'Power'), originally from Brittany.

In the Middle Ages the Templars' estate stretched almost as far as Guiting Power because the names of both Kineton (*Kinton* – once the king's manor) and Barton (*Berton* – a barn for barley or just an outlying farm) were listed in the Templars' records in the 1100s. At that time the Templars also held Naunton (*Niwetone* - the new farmstead or village). Naunton was very unusual at the time of Domesday Book in 1086 because part of it was held from the king by a nun, called *Cwenheld*. Our trip down the Windrush brings us to Bourton on the Water; *Burchton* in 714AD. The name means 'the settlement by the camp '- the camp being the Iron Age fort at

Bourton with its tourists and the River Windrush

Salmonsbury, just to the east of the village, which is more than two thousand years old. With its modern information panels, it is well worth a visit.

Lower Slaughter: no longer a muddy place

There is no need to search for the site of a bloody battle along the River Eye in the next valley to the Windrush. The name Slaughter comes from *Sclostre*, which is the same word as Slough, and means a muddy place; no doubt a vivid description of the valley bottom before a channel was created to allow the water to run through what is now the picture postcard village of Lower Slaughter. Both Slaughters were first recorded in Domesday Book.

I next turned my attention to the villages lying to the south of Guiting Power. Hawling was first recorded in 816AD as *Hallinge*, probably meaning 'the land between two valleys'. In contrast with today, this part of the Cotswolds must have been extensively wooded in the early Middle Ages, for the names of three neighbouring villages all refer to trees. Salperton (*Salpretune* in Domesday Book) was 'a/the farmstead where sallows, or willows', grew. Notgrove, 'a wet grove', was first recorded as *Notangratum* in the early 700s – it has nothing to do with nuts. Hazleton (*Hasedene* in Domesday Book) was 'a/the farmstead near the hazels'. One

Hazleton church and rectory

more village name deserves mention – Turkdean. It is the only one of all these local place names to feature the British language, for all the others come from Old English. 'Twrch' is modern Welsh for a boar and was probably the nickname given to the wild stream in the valley, so giving *Turcandene* by the early 700s. The dene came from *denu*.

Finally, after this brief tour of the north Cotswolds, what of the town which promotes itself as the centre for the Cotswolds? Cheltenham was first recorded in 803AD as *Celtanhomme*. Place name experts agree that *homme* means a water meadow but they cannot agree on the meaning of *Celtan*. They do agree, however, that the River Chelt is named from the

This early twentieth-century postcard emphasises the valley in which Turkdean lies

settlement and not vice-versa, as it was called the Arle Brook in the 13th century. The most recent research suggests *Celtan* could come from an old British word which means hill, which also appears in Chiltern. In which case Cheltenham could mean 'the water meadow by the hill'.

These place names suggest that by 700AD, English had probably become the dominant language in this part of Gloucestershire. Until the early years of the last century, the predominance of Old English names in the landscape had led historians to conclude these were all settlements newly created by the Anglo-Saxons. Archaeologists have shown conclusively that settlements had been established long before their names first appear. As I conclude this chapter on place names, I wonder how many readers have noticed that so many of our local place names, especially on the Cotswolds, are based on landscape features rather than personal names? They shout out the importance of the landscape and its resources to our ancestors over a thousand years ago.

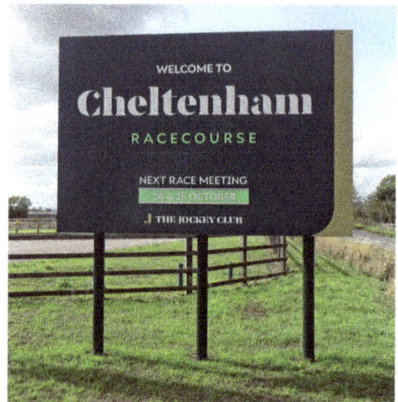

PLACES

History beneath our feet
in Bishop's Cleeve

It is true to say that people have very mixed feelings about the expansion of Bishop's Cleeve in recent years but what cannot be argued against is the enormous amount of archaeological evidence which has come to light as a result. In this article, which I wrote in June 2010 when the Directory covered only Bishop's Cleeve, I showed that the village has a long history going back over 4000 years.

O F ALL THE developments in the village since the building of the bypass in 1991, the arrival of Tesco was probably the most hotly debated, yet here the archaeologists found arguably the most valuable evidence of all. During the Bronze Age 4000 years ago the area was marshland. This meant that in the wet conditions enough pollen and seed survived to paint a picture of a landscape already largely cleared of trees and bushes and where the inhabitants were keeping animals and growing grain. It was a picture which did not change dramatically until the last century. From *c.*600BC attempts were made to drain the marsh by digging ditches and dumping waste, including bone needles and an antler comb, pottery, weights from a weaving loom and a whetstone for sharpening metal tools. A single post hole, now under Aisle 15 in Tesco, suggested a dwelling which meant people could have been living here over two and a half thousand years ago. The foundations of two large timber and thatched roundhouses dated to the Middle Iron Age (*c.*400BC – *c.*100BC) confirm people were living here before the Roman invasion of 43AD. Today Tesco's customers drive over the site of the round houses as they enter the carpark.

The entrance to Tesco carpark where two Iron Age houses were found

Leaving Tesco and crossing Church Road to Gilder's Paddock, we come to another important archaeological site, first excavated in 1989 by the county council's archaeological unit. The excavators found a very complicated pattern of ditches which suggested small paddocks for keeping animals. The ditches dated mostly from the Iron Age, from *c.*400BC to *c.*100AD. Fragments of pottery from Malvern and salt containers from Droitwich indicated links to the wider world.

At Dean's Lea or Greenacres to the north of the village centre came actual evidence of an Iron Age farmstead and this allowed the archaeologists from Birmingham University to give us an idea of the sort of buildings which were scattered around the landscape at that time. We should imagine the whole area around Bishop's Cleeve dotted about with such farms at the time of the Roman invasion in 43AD. The arrival of Roman influences seems to have had little direct effect on the way most people lived. It's only because the pottery changes in style and material that we can identity farmsteads as belonging to the Romano-British years (43AD - *c.*450AD) rather than the Iron Age. As a result we

Artist's impression of the Dean's Lea Iron Age farmstead (Birmingham University)

know that the ditches and other features found on Lidl's site were from this later period because Gilder's Paddock site was gradually abandoned by *c.*150AD. It later became a small cemetery, for seven graves were found there in 1989.

When the bypass was built, at least four or five more Romano-British farmsteads were discovered along its route, confirming that 2000 years ago our area was being densely farmed. There even seems to have been a Roman villa somewhere near Cleeve Hall. Although the actual location remains a mystery, bits of painted plaster from walls, luxury pottery and tiles from a hypocaust central heating system were found

One of the skeletons found during the building of Gilder's Paddock

scattered over a wide area. Another continuing mystery is why after c.400AD the farmsteads seem to have gone into decline.

From that period until our first written document, the charter granting the profit from an estate to St Michael's church in 777-79AD, we depend upon the archaeologists. Many sherds of Anglo-Saxon pottery were found on the Tesco site and the remains of a timber building were found in 1997 when Stoke Park Close was being built. Also a small cemetery from the late 500s, discovered near Stoke Road in 1989, provide clues that families continued to live here after the end of the Roman period.

Gotherington: an Ordinary Village?

When the village's local history society was founded in 1981, it was not unusual to hear the assertion, "Gotherington is just an ordinary village, it doesn't have a history!" This was a challenge which spurred the society's members to write a history. The first edition appeared in 1993 and a fully-revised second edition in 2012. Here is its abbreviated story.

GOTHERINGTON LIES AT the foot of the Cotswold scarp beneath Nottingham Hill. As I explained above, its name means 'Guthere's farmstead' and this was probably first used about 1200 years ago in Anglo-Saxon times, although it was not written down until Domesday Book in 1086. We have no idea who *Guthere* was, but it is likely his farmstead was the forerunner of the manor house which still overlooks the village from the lower slopes of Nottingham Hill. From Domesday Book we can work out that about a dozen slaves lived in a small settlement below the manor house in the area cut by the railway when it was built in 1906. This area was known as Upper Gotherington. There also existed a Lower Gotherington around Shutter Lane at the other end of the village, which was hidden in the Domesday entry for Bishop's Cleeve. Here lived the servants, both active and retired, of the Bishop of Worcester from where they attended to his manor house, now Cleeve Hall in Bishop's Cleeve. Not until the 20th century did new housing completely fill the gap between Upper and Lower Gotherington and create the shape of the modern village.

This small pond is the only surviving part of a moat dating back to c.1300 which once surrounded today's Moat Farm in Lower Gotherington

For two thousand years agriculture remained the bedrock of the village, with a small number of village craftsmen, such as blacksmith, carpenter and wheelwright. During the Middle Ages over 600 years ago, wives brewed ale and were often fined for selling it without a licence. The corrugated pattern of the medieval ridge and furrow which indicates ploughed land, still survives in places and some of the oldest houses in the village date back to before 1550. Baldwin's farmhouse in Gretton Road dates from the first half of the 14th century and Shady Nook in Shutter Lane dates from

The cruck frame exposed when Shady Nook in Shutter Lane was being re-built in 1989 dates back to the 1300s

the middle years of that century. In the 19th century two great changes affected the village; an act of parliament in 1807 resulted in the creation of the fields we see around the village today and in 1894 the manor estate, based on Upper Gotherington and which could be traced back to Domesday Book, was broken up into individual farms as agriculture suffered from foreign competition. In 1906 the railway arrived but times were hard for the villagers and many people left, even emigrated, to find a better life and yet traditional ways of living still continued into the middle years of the last century.

The beautifully restored Gotherington station of 1906 stands on the left and the Gloucestershire Warwickshire Steam Railway's halt on the right

It was the post-war years which brought the beginning of today's village. New houses were built for incoming workers at GCHQ, Smith's and Dowty's. Many were built in the orchards and fields as agriculture declined until today only one working farm remains. In the present century new estates have been built off Gretton Road, Malleson Road and Ashmead Drive as the village continues to attract families seeking its pleasant rural location. The incomers have stimulated a lively village social life. The long-standing WI was formed in 1953 and many other societies followed, including the local history society in 1981. Today there are over a dozen different groups and societies who meet regularly, details of which can be found on the village's website.

Simple Pleasures a Century ago – Eversfield Tea and Pleasure Grounds

I doubt that today many people still possess a piece of souvenir crockery inscribed 'A Present from Bishop's Cleeve'. There might be a scratching of heads regarding its origin as the village does not spring readily to mind as a tourist destination. Yet in the years between the two world wars it was very much a place to visit.

THE EVERSFIELD TEA and Pleasure Grounds began as the brainchild of Andrew Denley from Foxcote near Andoversford, who in 1898 bought a bakery with extensive orchard grounds bordering on what became Station Road. Ever an entrepreneur, Andrew purchased some secondhand seesaws and swings from a playground in Charlton Kings, which he installed in the orchard. He also converted an existing Dutch

Well-dressed children lead a party down Station Road to Eversfield Pleasure Grounds

barn into a tea room, in order to serve refreshments to the visitors. Andrew particularly wanted to attract respectable groups, especially church groups, rather than individuals: Cheltenham Parish Church Sunday School and Bible Class members, Charlton Kings Parish Church Guilds, and Hatherley and Reddings Band of Hope and Temperance Society were just three of the groups which visited in the early days. The First World War dampened demand and so it was in the inter-war period that the Pleasure Grounds really flourished. In his history of his family's venture, on which much of this article is based, David Denley, Andrew's grandson, drew a map showing the extensive area from where the groups came. At first it was always by train, with the recommendation that

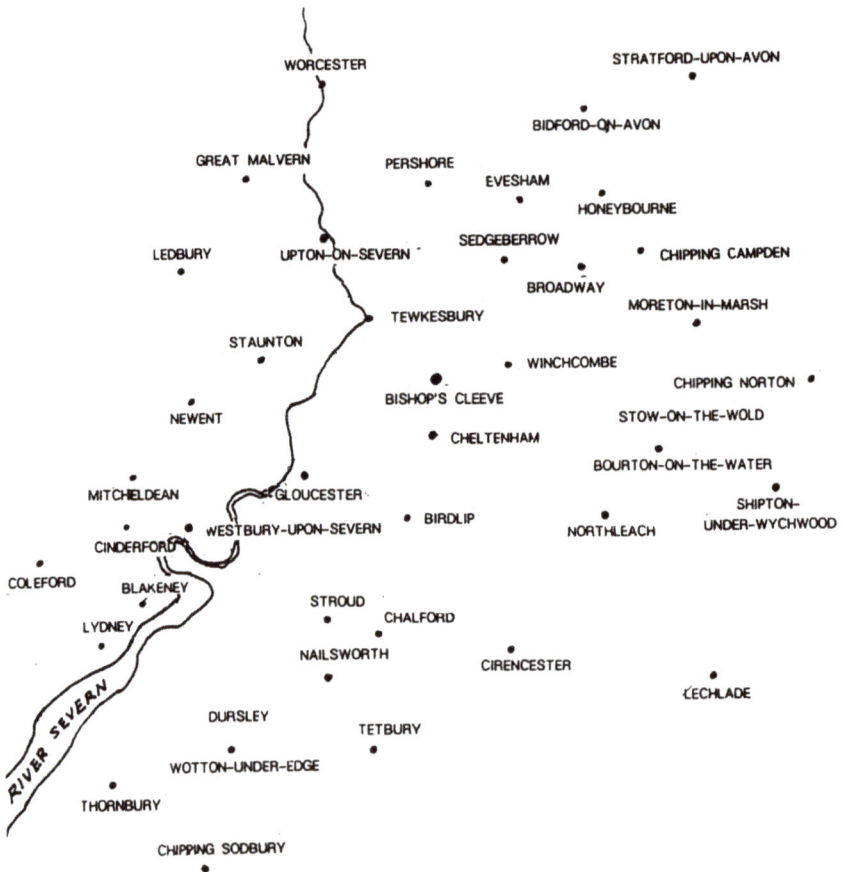

This plan taken from David Denley's book shows the widespread origins of the visitors to the Pleasure Grounds

parties of over 200 charter their own, but after the Great War visitors increasingly came by charabanc and this created real parking problems along Station Road.

The war having ended in 1918, the next year marked a re-launching of the Pleasure Grounds. We can learn from the publicity brochure that Eversfield 'should in no way be thought similar to the ordinary "pleasure garden"'. However, nearly a century later we might wonder how the visitors gained so much enjoyment from the rather primitive amusements on offer. These included a large wooden slide for adults and a smaller slide for children (regularly rubbed with paraffin wax to avoid too many splinters); a circular railway 30 feet in diameter on which two trucks were pushed around by the visitors themselves; a sloping railway 25 feet long with a truck which had to be similarly pushed back to the top; a miniature big wheel which could accommodate eight adults or children; a simple zip wire; a small roundabout, swings and a sea swing. This latter was a suspended square wooden crate which could be pushed in all directions, thus creating the impression of a rough sea, often leading to similar consequences!

A slide and the self-propelled railway

Once visitors had tired themselves out on the amusements, or in playing tennis or enjoying games and races in other parts of the grounds, they could sit down to eat 'a good plain tea' provided for parties at the special price of 9d (4p) per head, with white, brown and currant bread and unlimited cakes. Cheaper teas could be provided at 6d (2½p) per head and better class teas 'at moderate prices'. The cost of the tea of 3d (1p) was included in the admission. The Dutch barn soon became inadequate and so two tents were purchased where 600 people could sit down for their refreshments.

With the post-war re-start for the Pleasure Grounds came a new slogan 'A Square Deal and A Square Meal' and a new brochure, which promised 'only one party (if 200 or over) will be booked on the same day except with mutual consent'. Eversfield became increasingly popular and so the destruction of the Dutch barn in a fire in 1921 provided an opportunity to expand. In its place a permanent brick-built hall with a stage was erected. This also served as a village hall when the grounds closed for the winter. Ice cream and lemonade were made here by hand but the sticks of Bishop's Cleeve rock were made in Gloucester.

As the 1920s progressed new ways of attracting visitors were explored. The Humpty Dumpty cart seemed a good idea. It carried two adults or three children and was pushed by two men. If you are wondering how it gained its name, the axle was attached to both wheels one foot from their centre. It soon proved so dangerous it was normally

This postcard gives a good view of the extensive site

ORTION OF EVERSFIELD TEA GARDEN'S

kept locked up when not in use. Then there was the Flying Dutchman - a seesaw which also rotated around its centre. Eversfield seemed to specialise in attractions designed to make its visitors queasy. Modern health and safety regulators would take a very dim view of the higher and larger wooden slide which replaced the gently inclined do-it-yourself railway. Photographs show there were no safety rails, only netting to keep spectators at a distance. However, serious accidents seem to have been remarkably rare.

EVERSFIELD GARDENS   BISHOPS CLEEVE

Children in their Sunday best pose for the photographer

During the 1930s Alick Denley, who since 1921 had been in partnership with Charles Wright after his brother George had left to run a bakery in Gloucester, continued to develop the attractions. Two donkeys, one black and the other white were bought to give rides to the young visitors. An outside stage was constructed where for a small sum visitors could enjoy a Pierrot show and later in the decade wonder at 'Professor Garrard', a conjuror accompanied by his wife, who both dressed in Chinese costumes. In that pre-television age they must have provided quite a spectacle. Nearly all the attractions were free once the admission price had been paid. However it did cost 1d to ride on the hand-cranked miniature roundabout. Alick's son David writes that he did not enjoy turning the handle. He rather more willingly helped to bring bags of coconuts from the railway station for the coconut shy, where one ball cost 1d and seven cost 6d (2½p) which ironically was the price to buy one anyway.

The 1930s also brought electricity which made the catering much easier, especially making the ice cream, but on the other hand the decade also saw an increasing problem - parking and road congestion in Station Road as more groups came by charabanc. Part of the grounds had to be converted into a small carpark. Eversfield continued to be a popular destination right up to the outbreak of war in 1939.

However, at the end of the war six years later the attractions had suffered badly from neglect and the post-war years promised to be very different from the inter-war years. Although it was a sad decision, it was not a difficult one to make and so Alick Denley sold up, leaving only the original bakery attached to Eversfield House which continued until 1986. Today modern housing covers the site and no clues remain of this remarkable attraction which brought thousands of visitors to Bishop's Cleeve in the first three decades of the last century.

'EVERSFIELD GARDENS'

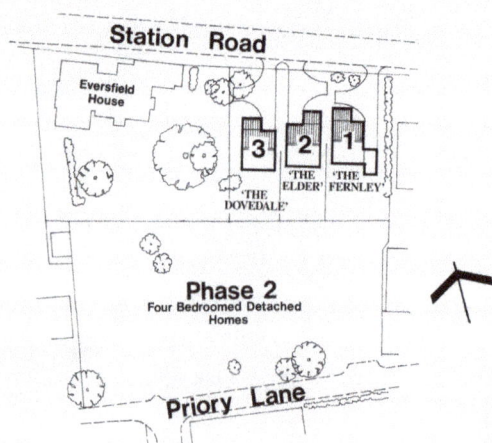

Clifton Homes traded on the Eversfield name when they developed part of the site in the 1980s

From Southam House to the Ellenborough Park Hotel

Southam House is one of the most prestigious buildings in the area covered by this book. In the July 2011 directory I wrote about the transformation of the former Hotel Delabere in Southam into the five star Ellenborough Park Hotel, having had access to the extensive alterations which enabled me to write a short history of the building for future guests. Twelve years later a tree-ring dating project carried out by the Gloucestershire Building Recording Group caused me to re-think the building's early history.

Southam House, now the Ellenborough Park Hotel. The Great Hall sits back from left of centre to the porch with its closed door

I BEGAN MY ORIGINAL article by explaining how the story started about the year 1500 when a local farmer and land owner, Thomas Goodman, decided to move from the old manor house (now Pigeon House) and build Southam House on a nearby green field site. However,

This oak truss above the Great Hall was tree-ring dated to 1316-17 in 2023 (A.Moir)

the tree-ring dating project discovered that the roof over the main hall, which extended from the two storey former porch on the left to the large oriel windows on the right, was dated 1316-17 and the wing running back from the oriel windows had timbers dated between 1322 and 1354. So it was obvious that Thomas Goodman had taken over a prestigious existing building. He did make several changes including extending the great hall to include the now-closed porch and

The Tudor rose in the bay window of the restaurant suggests this part had been built by 1509

installing stained glass in the oriel windows of the south wing. It is quite possible that he didn't finish his venture because within ten years he had sold it to Sir John Huddleston, the constable of Sudeley Castle. Sir John, or his son, also confusingly called Sir John, greatly enlarged the house to

Lord Ellenborough's Indian Memorial. There is a copy of my research into the names on the memorial in Bishop's Cleeve library

surround a courtyard which is now mostly filled by the modern atrium. Guests still remark on the impressive black and white timber framing which has survived nearly five hundred years. In 1554 son Sir John's daughter Eleanor married Kinnard de la Bere from Herefordshire and they and their descendants added more rooms to the south (to the right in the main picture). This was the house which George III visited during his stay in Cheltenham in 1788.

However, many readers will associate Southam House more closely with Edward Law, Earl of Ellenborough, who bought it in 1833 and it is this link which has provided the distinctive name for the new hotel. He added three towers including the impressive mock-Norman tower which can be seen from the road, two porches and an extensive stable block, in addition to remodelling the existing buildings. In the grounds he built an unusual memorial to those who helped him govern India (badly according to many people) from 1842-44 during a difficult time in that country's history. However, mention his name in local circles even today and he is remembered more for his private life than his public one. His first marriage ended in tragedy when his wife, Lady Octavia Stewart, died after only six years of marriage. His second marriage to the 'scandalous society beauty' Jane Digby had lasted only two years when she fled with an Austrian prince before finally settling down with an Arab chief. The Earl was then hit by a second tragedy when their son Arthur died aged only two. Yet he recovered. The census of 1871, the year in which he died, recorded the eighty one year old living in Southam House with three illegitimate daughters, Eva (18), Ellen (15) and Agnes (12) by two different mothers, plus seventeen servants and a governess. His son Edward Richmond, also illegitimate, a captain in the Hussars, was away at the time of the census.

By the end of that year the household split up. His house and lands were put into a trust, with the house passing to Edward. The trust remained intact until 1927 and in 1947 the house became the Oriel School for Girls for twenty five years before it was sold to become the Hotel Delabere. That closed in 2008 after which it was transformed into the Ellenborough Park Hotel.

A Common for All?

I wrote several directory articles on Cleeve Hill and its common. The following is a compilation of those articles, which ranged from the Middle Ages until the last century.

The stone described in the text

I F YOU WALK up Rising Sun Lane, turn right in front of the trees and almost immediately ascend the small hillock on the left you will find a bench. By it stands a stone with a very faint reversed 'S'. Make your way carefully down the opposite side of the raised ground and you will find another stone about 100 yards away. These particular stones are the best preserved of a number of stones which can still just be seen on the common. They were boundary stones. What boundary you might ask? The fading inscription itself provides the answer, for it represents a capital 'S', carved back to front by a stone mason not too sure of his letters. 'S' stands for Southam and it marks one side of the now long-forgotten boundary between the medieval manors of Bishop's Cleeve and Southam, meandering across the common from the top of Rising Sun Lane to the south-west edge of Postlip Warren. The boundary itself was first described in 1482, but the stones are much more recent, probably set up when Lord Ellenborough bought Southam manor in 1833. They divided the common into two unequal parts; two thirds to Southam manor and one third to Bishop's Cleeve manor. And therein lay many problems.

This next boundary stone is placed a little away from the historic manorial boundary

The common has always been valuable grazing pasture. It has been calculated that *c.*1400 sheep were grazing five to each of the common's thousand acres, in addition to untold numbers of cattle (said to have numbered 1500 in 1594), horses, donkeys and even chickens and geese. The problems stemmed from the fact that there were many more farmers in Bishop's Cleeve, but they had only half the area belonging to much smaller Southam and animals never did understand the need to keep to their side of the boundary.

In 1539 Sir John Huddleston of Southam House successfully prosecuted Richard Southall of Woodmancote, which was part of Bishop's Cleeve manor, for trespassing with over two hundred sheep and cattle on the Southam part of the common. In May 1593 and again in June 1594 the tenants of Southam accused the tenants of Bishop's Cleeve of the same trespass. Another problem at this time was caused by 'strangers', i.e. farmers living outside Bishop's Cleeve, buying both small plots of land in the village and also the rights from individual villagers to pasture their animals on the common. As late as November 1770 a farmer from Winchcombe, Henry Harvey, appeared before the manor court of Southam accused of putting stock on the common for which he

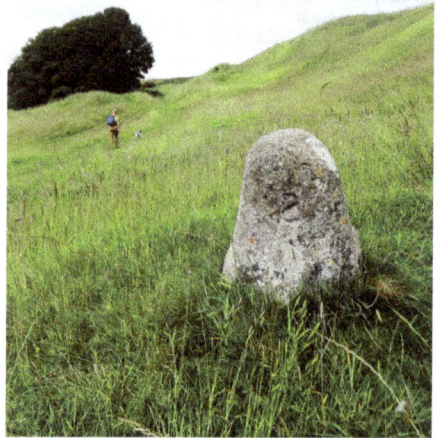

had no right at all. These recorded cases must have just been the tip of the iceberg.

So when did these struggles come to an end? By the time Lord Ellenborough came on the scene the villagers of Bishop's Cleeve were already beginning to control their uses of the common through the vestry - the forerunner of the Parish Council, so that when his lordship defined the boundary the conflicts were fast becoming history. Commissioners from the Ordnance Survey arrived in 1880 and again in 1882 to define the parish boundaries and they placed the whole of the common in Southam parish, where it remains to this day.

Sheep on Cleeve Common being driven up from the Washpool sometime in the 1930s (T.Curr)

So the next time you walk across the common, seek out the old boundary stones and reflect on a tumultuous episode in the history of this seemingly peaceful upland pasture.

Having written this article, several people asked me about the boundary and so this is what I wrote in reply.

Southam has been a manor since at least 991, but the earliest description we have of the boundary is from much later, from 1482:

> And so to a way called *Smale Way*..... following the same way eastward as it leads to *Birkmore* to the Cross Way there, and hence eastward as *staere waie* leads to *Chappmandeane* so forward to *potteslip* quarry.

We can actually follow the boundary quite easily. Today we know the *Smale Way* (narrow way) as Two Hedges Road and Gambles Lane. The modern boundary between Woodmancote and Southam still follows Gambles Lane for much of its line. *Birkmore* was the name of a field towards the top of Gambles Lane, remembered today in the house name *Bittemoor*. The Cross Way indicates the junction of Rising Sun Lane and Spring Lane (the present road was not built until 1823). For some reason the surviving boundary stones do not quite follow the *staere waie* up to

The Cross Dyke runs diagonally across this view of the hill

the top of the hill. The 'stair way' is the name which was given to the Cross Dyke climbing obliquely southwards up the scarp. Towards the top of the scarp it turns sharply north eastwards towards Postlip. The Cross Dyke fades away as it reaches the upper part of Dry Bottom. We know that the boundary followed it because it is still just possible to find the remains of two boundary stones along its length. Archaeologists have long been puzzled about its origins and at present they seem to think it dates from the Bronze Age (*c.*2,500BC to *c.*800BC). Even that long ago people were creating boundaries over Cleeve Hill.

The Tower House in Rising Sun Lane

In 1482 Dry Bottom was known as *Chappmandeane* ('the valley of the travelling merchant'). This might seem an odd name for this remote area of the common, but it indicates the very early route way which had come up from Queenwood in Prestbury and then went down to Postlip and Winchcombe. From the valley the boundary ran first northeastwards, to a stone in Postlip (*potteslip*) quarry, before running southeastwards to the present parish boundary as it ran towards Padcombe Bottom and then around Wontley and back along the southwest wall of West Down.

The King's Beeches

    Conflicts over the boundary were not confined to trespassing sheep. After Lord Ellenborough had purchased Southam House in 1833 he was determined to re-instate traditional ways, including beating the bounds every seven years. Giles Carter's Tower House in Rising Sun Lane had been built on the boundary between Bishop's Cleeve and Southam. In 1855 the bounds' beaters found the owner away and convinced the boundary ran through his house, forced their way in through a window and out through the door. At the next manor court held by Lord Ellenborough in Southam, Giles was forced to sign a statement promising he would always be at home when the perambulations took place.

    The use of the common's upland pasture for grazing was one of the two most important uses in the past, the other was the quarrying of the underlying limestone. This industry was an ancient one, for the story starts in Roman times at the King's Beeches at the top of Rising Sun Lane. It was here in 1902 that archaeologists found an Iron Age settlement lying under quarry waste in which they found three Roman coins from the 3rd century A.D. We also know that in Roman times there was a farmstead at nearby Haymes, where stone from the hill had been used for the footings of the walls. Succeeding centuries saw the scarp around Cleeve Cloud being transformed from a gentle slope to vertical cliffs. Seen from the air it is as if a gigantic mouse had eaten into a gigantic piece of cheese. From here came the good quality building stone, called freestone, which was used in Bishop's Cleeve's ancient buildings; St Michael's church from the 12th century, Cleeve Hall from the 13th century and the Tithe Barn from the 14th century. On the far northern side of the common we know that from before 1400 to 1539 the Abbot of Winchcombe was renting Postlip Quarry from the lord of the manor, the Bishop of Worcester, for a token annual rent of 6d (2½p). Most of the stone used in Winchcombe, including St Peter's church came from here. When the buildings of Winchcombe Abbey were demolished after its dissolution in 1539 the stone was re-used around the town. A document of 1529 tells us that each farmer in Bishop's Cleeve had to provide five wagonloads of stone every year for the upkeep of the roads. This reminds us that not all the quarries provided valuable freestone for buildings. They also provided grit and sand and along the Undercliff on the way to Nutterswood remains of limekilns have been found, where stone was burnt into lime for mortar.

As we reach the 19th century more details emerge of the industry. In 1832 Henry Gaskins, who probably lived at Laburnum Cottage, paid

Postlip Quarry

The Iron Age camp or hillfort. The quarrying was destroying the far ditch and banks

Lord Ellenborough, who as Lord of the Manor held the right to the minerals on the common, £20 a year to work the quarries. The 1851 census tells us that ten stonemasons were living in Bishop's Cleeve and Woodmancote. In 1878 the first explosives were used, in Milestone Quarry alongside the main road. In 1900 eleven quarries were still being worked, but their days were numbered, and not only because bricks were much cheaper and more convenient. In 1890 an act was passed which regulated the uses of the common, giving the Board of Conservators a mandate to protect and conserve the common. In 1911 local businessman and quarryman Arthur Yiend was ordered to stop quarrying along the face of Cleeve Cloud because he was destroying the Iron Age camp there. How much of this ancient monument has been destroyed by quarrying can be judged from the writings of

Samuel Rudder, the Gloucestershire historian, who wrote in 1779 that the entrance to the camp lay at the front overlooking the vale. So, as conservation became increasingly important, quarrying ceased in 1941. Freestone Quarry above the golf clubhouse was the last to be worked. Wickfield Quarry has been turned into the car park at the end of the lane to the golf clubhouse where you might leave your car for a walk across the common.

The act which was passed in 1890 was preceded by an enquiry into the uses of the common. The published minutes provide an insight into the increasing pressures on the common which the act was intended to regulate. They make interesting reading, informing us of the perceptions and prejudices of those people with an interest in this upland pasture. Colonel N.B. Thoyts, the mayor of Cheltenham, described Cleeve

Wickfield Quarry in 1901. It is now a car park

Common as the town's lungs and free breath. The free access enjoyed by the people of the spa town was increasingly resented by the local commoners who were concerned that the increasing recreational use of the common was interfering with their right to graze their animals on the common. As a result of the enquiry the act was passed under the

This forbidding notice stood at the Stockwell Lane entrance to the common for many years. Clause 3 prohibits the committing of 'any nuisances'. What might that mean?

long-winded title of Commons Regulation (Cleeve) Provisional Order Confirmation Act which set up the Board of Conservators, renamed the Cleeve Common Trust in 2017, which still administers the common today.

The common had been used by the people of Bishop's Cleeve, Woodmancote and Southam as pasture for their sheep, cattle, horses and donkeys for centuries, but when Cheltenham races were held on the hill, principally between 1819 and 1842, they left a legacy of race horse training, with the horses being brought up from Prestbury, but the trainers there had no rights on the hill. This encouraged a few of the local commoners to extort payments (£40 a time was mentioned at the enquiry) from the trainers to compensate for damage caused by the horses "galloping by like a whirlwind", sometimes as many as ten in a line. Even riders of horses using the common for pleasure were charged £5. These illegal payments were said to have been subsequently spent in the public house. The members of parliament on the committee did not flinch to label these actions as blackmail which needed stamping out.

All the witnesses at the enquiry agreed that the uses of the common needed regulating, but they disagreed about the method. Ironically the two witnesses most opposed to the proposals did not live locally. Arthur Heavens-Smith lived in Cheltenham (he had previously lived in Winchcombe) and William Etheridge, although he came from a local family, kept a public house in London. They were both commoners because both owned freehold land in the villages at the bottom of the hill which gave them the right to pasture as many animals on the common in the summer as their land would support in winter. However, the chairman of the enquiry, Sir Walter Barttelot MP was less than impressed by their claims. Heavens-Smith claimed he could winter twenty 'young beasts' on his fifteen acres but Etheridge failed to explain how the third of an acre holding of one of his tenants could sustain nine sheep in winter.

The crucial point to which these two objected was the number of places on the proposed Board of Conservators allocated to Cheltenham, in return for the town council's annual contribution of £50 towards the

Sheep on the common today.

expenses of administering the common. £40 of this was proposed to pay for a haywarden, the forerunner of today's rangers, to safeguard the animals. If four were appointed, together with the two appointees of the Lord of the Manor who was the legal owner of the common, these six could block proposals from the other six conservators who represented the local commoners and who since 1894 have been nominated by the parish councils. In the end Cheltenham accepted three representatives, which decision being agreed by all allowed the chairman to recommend the act be passed. It still governs the uses of the common over a century and a quarter later, although Cheltenham's contribution to the running of the Trust has been lost somewhere along the way.

Sudeley before the castle

The original article was written in August 2012 to coincide with Sudeley Castle's celebrations of the 500th anniversary of the birth of Queen Katherine Parr. The story of Sudeley Castle is well-known, but what is far less well-known is the story of Sudeley before the castle.

WE KNOW PEOPLE have been living in the Sudeley area since prehistoric times as visitors to the castle will be aware from the displays of flint implements picked up from the fields in the late 19th century. However, we have to wait until Domesday Book of 1086 to discover that there was once a large settlement at Sudeley. Its lord was Harold, a young boy who was the great-nephew of King Edward the Confessor, whose death led to William the Conqueror invading England in 1066. The entry in Domesday Book in 1086 tells us that there were twenty families and fourteen slaves living there. There was extensive farmland and a very large wood which still survives today in patches like Spoonley Wood. Six mills were also listed, possibly on the Beesmoor Brook as well as on the River Isbourne. By 1175, when a chapel is referred to, a manor house had already been built. The two usually stood close together and so it is very possible that today the castle and St Mary's church stand on their original sites.

Two later tax records can tell us more about the village. In 1327 sixteen people were rich enough to pay the tax, including two

This print of 1789 shows the chapel where Queen Katherine Parr was buried in the centre of the illustration. It probably stands on the site of the village church. At that date it was a picturesque ruin.

millers. Historians think this means there might have been as many as forty families in the village as many were too poor to be taxed. The very unpopular Poll Tax of 1381 was meant to be paid by all adults and thirty five people paid a flat rate of one shilling (5p) each, which probably represented twenty families. Numbers had dropped since the Black Death, although Sudeley was still a sizeable village. In 1406 about fifteen families were still living there. By 1522 that number had reduced by half. The community continued to decline and in 1625 when there was a plan to merge the parishes of Winchcombe and Sudeley, it was reported

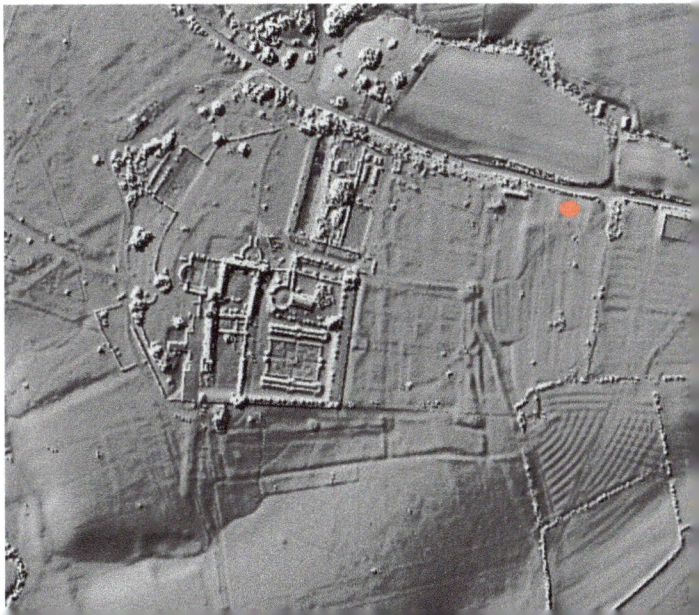

The lidar image shows the abandoned formal gardens of the castle with the ridge and furrow of medieval farming stretching around them. The 2024 dig site is marked in red (National Library of Scotland)

that only four families were living in the parish. So what might have caused this decline?

The short answer is that at present we don't really know, but we can make a suggestion. In 1442 Sir Ralph Boteler began his extensive rebuilding of the castle. Did he move the villagers away to create a deer park for hunting, as we know happened in other places? Some, if not all,

Foundations of a building in the village excavated in 2024 by archaeologists from DigVentures

must have moved into Winchcombe. However, if we can't yet be certain of the answer to this question, we are discovering where they might have lived.

Careful study of aerial photographs suggested part of the village at least might have stood on the southern side of the road leading up Sudeley Hill. In October 2024 DigVentures organised an archaeological dig and found many fragments of medieval pottery and even uncovered the foundations of a building which has been tentatively identified as

Boilingwell

a store room. Its position is in line with Boilingwell at the bottom of the hill. Future investigations could reveal that, although the present building is later, it represents the last house of the medieval village. You can read more about the findings on the DigVentures' website.

Hailes and Winchcombe Abbeys

I wrote three articles on the two local abbeys. Today the extensive remains of Hailes Abbey can be visited but what very little remains of Winchcombe Abbey lies in private grounds in the centre of the town. They both have interesting but very different stories to tell.

H AILES ABBEY WAS founded in 1246 by Richard, Earl of Cornwall and younger son of King John, to fulfil a promise he made to God when in danger of shipwreck in a storm near the Scilly Isles. Twenty monks came from his father's monastery at Beaulieu in Hampshire to organise the building of the abbey and five years later enough had been completed for the king and queen to attend a glittering ceremony to dedicate the abbey church.

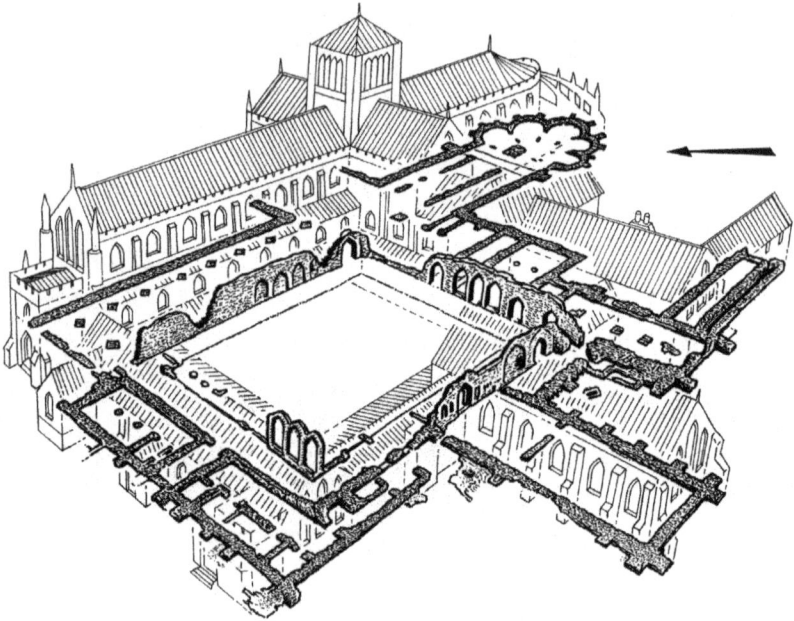

A modern impression of how the abbey might have looked based on the remaining features

Hailes was one of the last monasteries ever to be built and it never prospered until 1277 when Richard's son Edmund presented it with a small glass container said to contain Christ's blood spilt at the crucifixion. This revolutionised the abbey's fortunes. The church was enlarged with a shrine and right up until King Henry VIII closed the abbey on Christmas Eve 1539, it became a magnet for pilgrims. The faithful were told that visiting the Holy Blood would reduce their time in Purgatory, where they were punished for their sins before reaching heaven, by twenty two years.

We are fortunate to have a vivid account of what happened at the shrine, despite its being written by a sceptic at the end of the abbey's life. In modern English it reads as follows,

> At the shrine the priest showed the pilgrim a small glass container. One side had thick glass; the other much thinner glass. The thick side was shown until the pilgrim had paid enough money (for holy mass) as the priest thought fit. Then the thin side was shown so the blood could be seen, to the pilgrim's great joy.

This is the only known drawing of the tabernacle which housed the blood, but we are not sure of its accuracy

It was clear that the richer pilgrim, the more money the priest demanded.

However not everyone valued the experience. The pious pilgrim Marjory Kempe visited the abbey in the early 1400s and was appalled by the swearing and bad language of the monks who looked after the shrine. Sir John Drury, the vicar of Windrush near Burford, declared the relic was a fake and he had wasted 18d (7½p) on it when he visited in 1517. After the abbey had been closed, it was claimed to have been the blood of a drake or honey coloured with saffron.

Yet the story of Hailes Abbey does not end with its closure in

The Tracy's manor house drawn in 1732

The chapter house entrance before any archaeological excavation took place

1539. Part of it was converted into a country mansion where the Tracy family lived before they moved back to Toddington. By the end of the 18th century the whole site had become ruinous. In 1899 the first archaeological investigations took place and then conservation of the remains started in 1927, when the museum was opened and a halt built on the nearby railway to encourage visitors. The National Trust took over in 1948 and today it is managed by English Heritage, which continues to care for the site for ours and future generations to enjoy.

Think of Tewkesbury or Pershore Abbey and you will have an idea of the abbey which came to dominate Winchcombe. Today all obvious traces have

The nave of Winchcombe Abbey might have been similar to that of Tewkesbury Abbey, recorded in this nineteenth-century print

disappeared and its site lies in private gardens adjoining Abbey Terrace. It is doubly unfortunate because most of its written records were consumed by two fires, by the one in the town in 1151 and also in the Great Fire of London in 1666. There is also the added complication that the monks forged some of their documents to make up for the early losses.

The story possibly starts in the late 600s when a church for several priests was built in the town as part of an attempt to christianise the Hwicce; an early Saxon kingdom mostly covering Gloucestershire, Worcestershire and parts of Warwickshire, and of which Winchcombe was an important centre. The abbey's forged records suggest the famous King Offa of Mercia established a nunnery in 787 and that his successor, King Kenulf, founded an abbey in 797 which was dedicated in 811. We can be more certain that it became a Benedictine Abbey (as Gloucester and Tewkesbury) c.970. Henceforth it would have been a monastery as we think of them with monks living in an enclosed community. Domesday Book of 1086 recorded that its wealth was second in the county to St Peter's Abbey in Gloucester, now the cathedral. The abbey's wealth was largely based on its extensive landholdings, stretching mostly from Honeybourne in the vale to Bledington in the Cotswolds. During the next two hundred years it continued to increase its landholding so that when it was dissolved on 23rd December 1539, it was the tenth richest abbey in the whole of South West England.

During its lifetime it played a very important part in the life of the town and surrounding area. The number of monks varied between forty five in 1282 to twenty in 1423 and eighteen at the Dissolution, but they employed a large number of servants and craftspeople. On its closure, ninety were given a year's wages but the removal of such an important employer plunged the town into poverty for nearly a century.

Relationships with the town were not always cordial. In 1231 and again in 1399 the vicar was ordered to stop the deliberate ringing of the bells of neighbouring St Peter's church, timed to drown out the monks' worshipping. In 1346 and 1360 it was attacked and looted by local men. On the other hand, when St Peter's fell into disrepair about 1415, for a number of years the townspeople worshipped in the nave

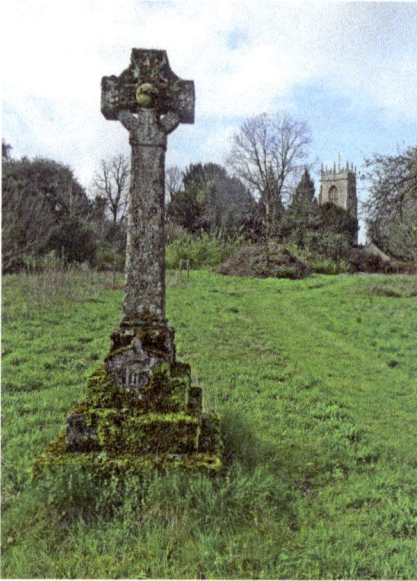

The cross erected by Emma Dent of Sudeley after the excavations of 1893 to show where the tower once stood

of the abbey church, until Abbot William led the rebuilding of the parish church with the financial help of the townspeople and Ralph Boteler of Sudeley. This, of course, removed any need to use the abbey church after the Dissolution, unlike Tewkesbury or Pershore, but similar to Evesham.

Finally, if Hailes had the Holy Blood to attract the pilgrims, Winchcombe had the legend of St Kenelm. Kenelm was the seven year old son of Kenulf who was murdered on the orders of his wicked sister Quendryth. In 1291 pilgrims were spared one year and

forty days in Purgatory if they worshipped on the feasts of St Kenelm (17th July) and the Virgin Mary (8th September) to whom the abbey was dedicated.

The legend can be summarised as follows: after the death in 821 of his father King Kenulf of Mercia, his seven year old son Kenelm became king, only to be murdered by his sister Quendryth whilst he was in the Clent Hills south of Birmingham. His body was later brought back to Winchcombe Abbey for burial. This story seems to have been corroborated when the

The image of St Kenelm at the well building on Sudeley Hill, paid for by Emma Dent

stone coffins of an adult and child were excavated in 1815 in the abbey grounds and the child's coffin included a knife. Was this the actual murder weapon? This seems all quite convincing until we dig below the surface and consult the archives. They tell us that Kenelm was a young man of about twenty five who died in about 811, before his father, and Quendryth, far from being the wicked sister was a nun and then an abbess. So the next question is, how might the legend have arisen?

The earliest surviving version of the legend dates from the early 1200s, perhaps based on an earlier story, but even this did not appear until probably two hundred years after the murder was supposed to have happened. The tale was most likely invented to encourage pilgrims to visit Winchcombe Abbey, especially on St Kenelm's day. Yet no shrine of the saint was ever recorded or found in the abbey. So what about the coffins? David Donaldson, in his history of Winchcombe, suggested they might have been buried by the monks to give support to the legend. The

The reputed coffin of St Kenelm drawn soon after its discovery in 1815

coffins can still be seen at St Peter's church, but the bodies and the knife are said to have crumbled to dust. The legend of St Kenelm provides a good story but so also does the search for the truth. Legends, myths and folk history can bring the past alive but investigating their origins can be even more interesting.

An amazing story of water and stone: Guiting Power Stone Pipe Company

In June 2014 Professor Hugh Torrens of Keele University filled Guiting Power Village Hall to recount a two hundred year old story of a company which used local stone to make pipes to carry water. At the time I felt it was a little known story so fascinating it had to be shared with a wider audience. Since then I have added to the original article through my own researches.

THE STORY BEGAN many miles away in the expanding cities of London and Manchester where rapid industrial growth was creating horrifically unhygienic conditions. At that time the responsibility of providing adequate water supplies fell to private companies, but they

An industrial scene in the Cotswolds. The company offices in the foreground and the houses of the workers in the distance. The works stood in the field on the opposite side of the road, now largely an orchard

had a problem. Pipes made from traditional elm soon rotted and iron pipes tainted the water and were expensive and difficult to make. Step forward Sir George Wright from Essex, who in 1805 obtained a patent to cut pillars and tubes from stone, which could then be turned into pipes to carry water. He first experimented with Portland stone from Dorset and small-scale trials proved successful. However, supplies of Portland dried up when King George III put an end to their use as pipes for water and so in 1806 Sir George set up his own company to look for alternative supplies. Unlikely as it now seems, his Stone Pipe Company decided to use Cotswold limestone, choosing a quarry near Guiting Power and setting up a factory in an adjacent field, bringing water from a tributary of the River Windrush and a conduit from nearby Cloud Hill. Samuel and Richard Hill, bankers from London, became partners and the new company became known as Hills' company.

Tally Ho quarry lies near the Cheltenham to Stow Road and is still marked on large-scale Ordnance Survey maps. Here the partners found Inferior Oolitic limestone which could be cut into pipes up to two feet across and fifteen feet long. Newly quarried it was much easier to work than Portland stone. In June 1810 the company advertised for workmen in the *Cheltenham Chronicle* and built houses for them, which still survive today. In the same year two fourteen horse power Boulton and Watt steam engines were delivered from Birmingham. Main pipes could be three to six feet long and were cut to be octagonal in shape. The circular core which was then cut out of the centre could be used for the smaller, lower pressure pipes.

By early 1812 thirty tons of pipes were daily or weekly (historians disagree) carried along the local roads, particularly the Stow turnpike road (now B4068); either westwards to the Cheltenham and Gloucester tramroad at Leckhampton for Gloucester docks and Manchester, or eastwards, probably to Radcot on the Thames, for London. At the same time, coal needed to run the engines was regularly being delivered from Gloucester and we can only imagine the state of the local tracks. In 1810 plans had been put forward for a sixty mile canal from the River Avon at Stratford to Abingdon on the River Thames, but existing canal companies objected. Then in 1811 a tramroad was proposed to meet the Gloucester and Cheltenham tramroad in Leckhampton, but local land owners, through whose land the route was planned, killed that idea. However, the

proposals did show that the partners were very aware of the transport problems.

For some lucky local people, the works provided alternative employment to agriculture, but it could be dangerous work. Guiting Power's burial register records two fatalities in 'Messrs Hills works'. In May 1811 nine-year-old Mark Waller was killed by a fall and nine months later William Cook fell through a trapdoor on the roof 'which had been carelessly left open' onto one of the steam engines. The *Cheltenham Chronicle* continued, 'His death by decapitation was a particularly grisly end'.

The major orders for the pipes came from London and Manchester, but some found their way to Dublin and even Eastnor Castle in Herefordshire which was being built at this time. Enough pipes for 41 miles was ordered for London. A special stone pipe wharf was set up on the Grand Junction canal in Paddington with a new reservoir and three and a half miles of main pipe were laid along Oxford Street towards New Bond Street. In June 1812 water started flowing from the reservoir but immediately it started to leak from the pipes; they were too porous to withstand the high pressure along the main artery. John Rennie, the famous civil engineer, who had advised the Stone Pipe Company in setting up its factory, was asked by the directors of the Grand Junction Waterworks, whose company had bought and laid the pipes, for a report. The following month this announced that 'the use of Stone Pipes for Mains cannot be continued'. There was considerable discussion whether they could still be used for the side branches where the water pressure was much less and so it wasn't until the following year that it was decided to abandon the whole project. The water company then tried to get its money back from the Stone Pipe Company and the company was forced to repay £23,000 from the original payment of £34,000. In future all the company's pipes would be made from metal.

In Manchester, the Manchester and Salford Water Works Company was set up in June 1809 to improve the water supply in the rapidly growing cities. Interestingly and perhaps significantly the directors included Samuel and Richard Hill of the Stone Pipe Company. The

opposite page: A modern interpretation of how the pipes were made showing the sophisticated boring machines driven by steam engines (Upper Windrush Local History Society)

following year the company started to lay 63 miles of pipe at a cost of
£95,000 and the two people most responsible for laying them down were
the Hill brothers. They laid the mains pipes in parallel streets but did not
join them up until the Water Works Company had completed a payment
of £36,984 to the Stone Pipe Company. This suggests they were already
aware of the leakages that would occur from the pipes when water was
sent under pressure along the whole system. On 10th or 11th July 1812
the water was turned on and 'the subengineer, Mr. Freemantle, turned
some water into a part of the 18-inch stone-pipe main, laid down near
the reservoir, and the main burst, although only a little pressure had
been laid on it'. The conclusion was the same as in London a month
earlier. Yet the stone pipes continued to be laid in low pressure areas,
although in September the Water Works Company stopped buying any
more stone pipes. It has been calculated that 53,000 pipes had been
sent to Manchester and so many went unused that the Water Works
Company had to dump them all in a big pit away from the city centre. The
Stone Pipe Company was sued and went into receivership with debts of
£81,500 (equivalent to £40 million today). This led to the failure of its
bank and so the debts were never paid and the partners fled abroad. In
1817 an act was passed that all water pipes had to be made of metal.

In July 1815 the works
and machinery were auctioned
off. One of the steam engines
was bought by the Stafford Mill
in Bowbridge near Stroud but
the fate of the second steam
engine and the machines used
in the process of making the
pipes is not known. Today there
is nothing to see on the site of
the factory, but the housing for
the workers and the company's
offices survive, as do many of

This pipe sample is on display in Manchester's Museum of Science and Industry

the unused pipes, which can be found built into the local Cotswold stone
walls. The Upper Windrush History Society's website has a much more
detailed history of this amazing venture.

Evidence of the venture can still be seen around Guiting Power as unused piping provided a ready source of material for Cotswold stone walls

'In the Valley of the Gods'

I enjoy browsing around secondhand bookshops. Imagine my delight when I came across a book of poems about our area.

IN THE VALLEY of the Gods was written in 1921 by William Vizard, a native of Winchcombe, and his 'valley' covered the Severn Vale, from the Forest of Dean to the Malverns and across to the Cotswolds. Today we might find much of the poetry sickly-sweet, written as it was between the end of the First World War and the hardships of the 1920s and 1930s. William's poetry speaks of a slower, gentler way of life when agriculture still formed the backbone of the villages, where towns like Winchcombe were both social and commercial centres, and stately homes were still important features in the landscape. Of course there is nothing of the grinding rural poverty, isolation and unhealthy housing conditions of the time. 'I have done my best,' writes the author in his introduction, 'but whether I have done well is another matter'. Our opinions might well be different from his contemporary readers. A flavour of the poetry can be gauged from this extract from the poem 'By way of Bushcombe Hill':

GOTHERINGTON.

From Woodmancote to Gotherington
Do hilly slopes abound;
From Woodmancote to Woolstone, there,
Are all with beauty crown'd.
Have I not trod these quiet ways
While merely yet a boy?
Have I not trod these pleasant ways
In early manhood's joy?
Have I not trod these peaceful ways
While in my manhood's prime?
Ah! yes; I have, morn, noon and night,
Full many and many a time.

William's pride in his native town is expressed in the introduction, 'Every cock can crow on his own fence' he wrote:

Give me a quiet old-world town,
Far from the crowded broad
     highway,
Somewhere within the sound of
     rills (i.e. streams),
Among the lovely peaceful hills,
All snugly tuck'd away;
Painswick, for instance, old
     Broadway,
Or Stow-upon-the-Wold:
But Winchcombe is, as you may
     hold,
Quiet and quaint, and very old,
And charming in her way:
As for this rock hewn, hill-born
     town,
I love her dear old-fashioned ways:
T'would give me ever sweet delight
To sing her lasting praise!

WINCHCOMBE.

Then there's Sudeley, where the
author's enthusiasm for the castle really took over:

Fair Sudeley! boast of all the plain;
Fair castle! Pride of Winchcombe still;
The Cotswolds noted will remain
As long as thou dost grace the hill.

But Hailes Abbey filled him with dread:

But thee, grim abbey, who art a wreck
Of the once noble self; how gaunt thou art:
Thou seems't a corpse, the death clutch at thy neck,
Lurid and stark, a dagger in thy heart:
Thou mak'st me shudder in the broad noonday:
Then would I, ere the eve comes, walk away.

Here a contrast with today's perceptions is startling. Today's visitors enjoy its peace and beauty.

To William Vizard Stanway House became a place of pilgrimage:

> But Elcho's home; - we will not pass it o'er,
> But pause and drink, - drink deep the lovely scene -
> Here will we play the votary, and adore
> A beauty spot of England, calm, serene!

No doubt William Vizard was hoping that the owners of Sudeley Castle and Stanway House, like the other stately homes described in his poems, would purchase at least one copy of his volume. However, he realised this would not be the case at Toddington Manor, which was sold by the 4th Lord Sudeley in 1893 due to bankruptcy. Today it is on the register of buildings at risk:

TODDINGTON MANOR.

> This is the great and grand estate
> That once an owner lost,
> All which a noble son gave up

At such tremendous cost,
From shame and degradation
His hapless sire to save.

William Vizard dedicated his poems to his wife Fanny 'as a mark of deep appreciation for her constant love and loyalty' and so let him have the last word here, in his poem HOME, SWEET HOME:

A faithful wife, a cheerful fire,
A dog, a purring cat,
A good old song, a merry tale,
A pleasant bit of chat,
All homely joys are born to please;
What worldly joys can equal these?

My copy had found its way to Liverpool. To its owner, the rural Severn Vale must have seemed a world away. To modern readers, the volume conjures a semi-fictional idyll of tranquillity and innocence of nearly a century ago.

A feature of the book is the large number of photographs which show our area c.1920. Here is just a small selection.

THE INN, BECKFORD.

TRANSPORT

The Story of our Roads

In September 2015 the Bishop's Cleeve and Winchcombe areas were beset with roadworks. This made me think at that time about the importance of our local roads.

M Y INVESTIGATIONS STARTED with a fascinating map from 1675 produced by John Ogilby. It was the first ever strip map covering the country's major roads. His road number 70 shows the route from Gloucester to Coventry, which passed through Cheltenham and

The construction of the Cleevelands roundabout on the A435 in Bishop's Cleeve which caused so much disruption in 2015

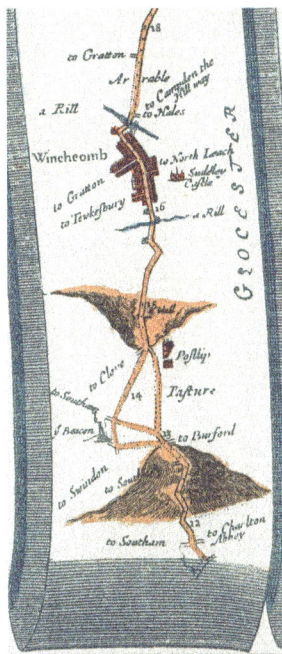

Ogilby's road map of 1675

Winchcombe. From Cheltenham it followed Prestbury Road to the village but from there it is difficult to identify exactly the route taken. It looks as if it reached Cleeve Common up Mill Lane. Ogilby gave advice for crossing the common 'by an irregular way over a hill a mile in height, by a beacon on the left.' The hill is certainly shown as steep on the map, but a mile high? Presumably the beacon stood near to where the trig point stands today. From the hill the route then dropped down through Postlip to Winchcombe. The map shows two routes across the common, the more westerly being along Dry Bottom which can still be followed. The eastern route has been destroyed by later quarrying. A contemporary of John Ogilby was Thomas Baskerville who wrote of his extensive travels around England. Here is his description of the route across the common:

Ogilby's western route came down from the sky line along the White Way, a prehistoric trackway running across the hill, and then turned down Chapmandean/ Dry Bottom towards Postlip

From the top of this high and aery becon hill the prospects are soe alluring and intermingled with so much variety, that as a man may say it may be like that with which the devil did tempt Christ, a shew of glory of the world and its riches.

The side roads in Winchcombe shown on Ogilby's map make for interesting reading: Malthouse Lane to Tewkesbury, Castle Street to Northleach and North Street to Gretton. The main route then took the traveller to Campden through Didbrook and Snowshill.

In 1759 the Royal Society of Arts offered £100 for the first accurate one inch to a mile map of every county. In 1775 Isaac Taylor submitted his map of Gloucestershire, and although the society decided his map was not accurate enough to win the prize, we can use it to discover the road from Cheltenham to Bishop's Cleeve nearly 250 years ago. It was very different and much longer than today's. It took the traveller through Prestbury to Southam, then down Southam Lane to Kayte Lane and into the centre of the village along a long lost track from opposite the end of Kayte Lane to St Michael's church. Readers might have noticed a remnant of it passing the entrance to Bishop's Cleeve primary school as Tobyfield Lane. One way to Gotherington is shown going from Woodmancote along Butts Lane: the other is the coffin path which now runs through the Homelands estate to Shutter Lane. Going west from Gotherington, the road shown passing the Elm is not the A435 but another lost route, barely traceable today, linking Pamington to Swindon Village.

Isaac Taylor's map of 1775

The 1792 turnpike road survives as the track running across the bottom of Cleeve Common and to the right of Cleeve Lodge

By 1775 our local road network had evolved over many centuries, mostly to meet the needs of villagers travelling short distance on foot or by horse. Within the next twenty five years this network was beginning to change significantly into our modern network. The reason? The growth of Cheltenham as a spa town and the subsequent increase in long distance travel.

When King George III stayed in the fledgeling spa town for six weeks in 1788 he put it firmly on the map. During his visit he travelled through Southam to Winchcombe and Sudeley and it cannot be coincidence that the route between Cheltenham and Winchcombe was greatly improved in 1792 when it became a turnpike road with the tolls being used to keep it in good repair. Tollgates were set up in Southam, near the New Road junction, and in Winchcombe, at the bottom of

Corndean Lane. Coaches, wagons, carts, travellers on horseback and farm animals made their way up and down what are now Spring, Lye and Ashleigh Lanes and then across Cleeve Common. This was less steep and certainly less wild than the road John Ogilby had depicted in 1675 running over the top of the hill, yet travellers still struggled along this new route and so in 1823 the road we now travel on was built, removing some of the worst gradients. This left a strip of land between the two roads ripe for development - but that is another story.

In the 1870s Edward Stevens' Broadway coach travelled the present Cleeve Hill road twice a week and changed horses at The George in Winchcombe

As Cheltenham rose in popularity, a new network of roads began to radiate from the town. Today they carry familiar names; Bath, Cirencester, London - and Evesham. Sitting in frustration in yet another queue at the Newlands, has it ever occurred why the crossroads exist at

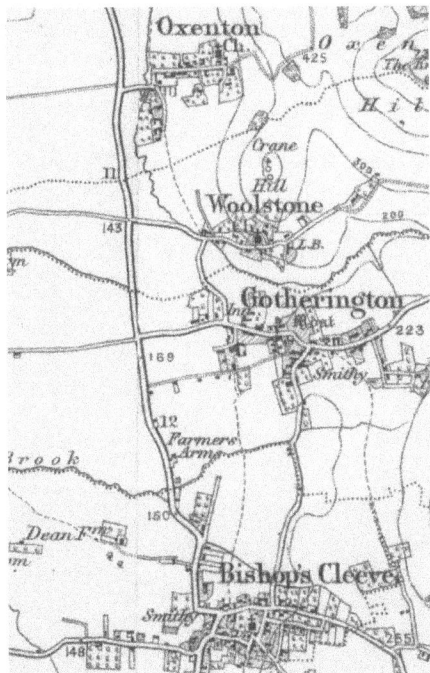

This Ordnance Survey map of 1900 shows how the 1807 turnpike road, now A435, crossed existing roads near Gotherington and Woolstone (National Library of Scotland)

all? Consider also the crossroads at New Barn Lane, Gotherington and Woolstone. They are clear evidence that the Evesham Road was a brand new road, crossing existing routes. We know it was built in 1807 and although its purpose was to link Cheltenham to Evesham, it proved a godsend for the people of Bishop's Cleeve as it made their trips to the shops and markets in Cheltenham so much easier. A planned new route to the north of the village was never built. Along the road which was built, Oxenton tollhouse still displays its flaking toll board, although travellers have not paid since 1877.

These routes to Winchcombe and Evesham still dominate transport in our area today but two more 19th-century changes are worth noting. In Winchcombe cars can be parked in Abbey Terrace because in 1837 the abbey grounds were cut back to their present line. The road around the car park was the original route here. Then if you have ever wondered why the Southam to Woodmancote road is called New Road, the answer goes back to 1879 when Lord Ellenborough reluctantly agreed to a new road replacing the earlier route arriving in Southam at what is now Ratcliff Lawns.

As long as road travel was based on the horse, then these roads sufficed, but the 20th century brought in the age of motor transport, which led to further changes. Tarmac was gradually laid down from the 1920s and in 1991 Bishop's Cleeve bypass was constructed. If each change was made to improve the traffic flow and if cynics say it encourages even more traffic, just remember how easy it is for local people to reach Cheltenham compared to 300 years ago.

Lifeblood of the Villages: Country Carriers

Having outlined the development of some of the local roads I later followed that up by considering some of the traffic which used them and then focussed on Cheltenham in 1880 – the heyday of the country carrier.

E ARLY IN 2017 a photograph of a small round thatched building at Seven Springs appeared in the *Gloucestershire Echo*. There followed lively speculations about its function; none of which was correct. This made me think at the time about an aspect of country life which has now all but faded from memory - the country carrier.

Few readers are likely to remember the country carrier, that essential link between the village and market town in an age when

The rebuilt parcel house

the railway brought goods to the towns and their shops but not to the surrounding villages lacking their own railway station. The typical carrier was a one person concern owning a horse and cart of various shapes and sizes who travelled to the nearest market town once, twice or three times a week, carrying the village shoppers and running errands for those who could not go themselves. So how does this link to the building standing at Seven Springs, known as the parcel house? It was there for the country carrier from North Cerney to Cheltenham to leave the parcels and newspapers to be collected by the good folk of Seven Springs for whom he ran errands. By good

The parcel house before it was rebuilt

fortune I had taken a photograph of it before the road junction was rebuilt several years ago and thankfully it was rebuilt and not demolished with the junction's re-modelling, even though it is not an exact replica.

The age of the country carrier lasted from the 1820s to the early 1950s. The main centre in the county was originally Gloucester, but when Cheltenham grew as a spa town with an increased number of shops, it too was a busy centre and became the destination of carriers serving the surrounding villages. At the height of the carriers' popularity in 1880, fifty different carriers operated one hundred and fourteen journeys each week into Cheltenham; each of them ending at one of ten of the town's inns and hotels. Almost all of them stood on the High Street, stretching from The Shakespeare (now The Shamrock) in the Lower High Street or West End, to The Old Swan (now The Swan) at the opposite end of the High Street. Fortunately both of these still survive, but nearly all the others have disappeared over the years as the town centre has been constantly redeveloped.

Not only did these inns provide a convenient drop off and pick up point for any passengers, but they provided the carrier with the facilities to park his cart, water and feed his horse and if he had few errands to distract him, enjoy the hospitality of the establishment whilst picking up juicy town gossip. On many occasions the fact that his horse knew its way home saved the carrier's reputation, even if on the climb to the Cotswolds above Charlton Kings or up to Seven Springs, the luckless passengers were expected to get out and push. In fact the carriers' carts were often so overloaded and underpowered that it was quicker to walk anyway.

In 1880 the fifty different carriers into and out of Cheltenham came from a wide area, from Broadway in the north to Northleach in the east, Cirencester in the south and Apperley in the west. Tuesdays, Thursdays and Saturdays were by far the most popular days with only Gloucester and Winchcombe enjoying a daily carrier service. In Cheltenham Thursday was (and still is) market day but it was the spa town's shops which provided the main reason for the Tuesday and Saturday visits.

So who were the carriers? We know from their names that all but two of them were men. It must have been relatively straightforward for the enterprising to set themselves up with a horse and cart, perhaps from a previous owner. This must have been quite common, for not a single carrier in 1880 had been operating in 1870 and a decade later

Although Wiggett's carrier's cart is recorded c.1870 linking Prestbury to Cheltenham, this photograph was taken outside the White Hart in Winchcombe (T. Petchey)

only George Troughton, who took over the George Inn in Winchcombe in 1885, and William Oldacre from Bishop's Cleeve were still operating. Both had another occupation, as did nearly all the other carriers. You couldn't make a living from being just a carrier.

The destination in the town was one of ten inns. They have practically all vanished and only The Old Swan in the Strand is still recognisable as a carriers' inn with a large gateway leading into its yard. It is not difficult to imagine the carriers emerging from that gateway during the late afternoon and setting off on their journey back to the Cotswold villages. In fact four o'clock on Thursday market day saw a mass departure of carriers from the inns of the town, similar to the 2pm departures from the Black and White coach station in St Margaret's Road almost a century later.

The Old Swan (now The Swan) in Cheltenham High Street, photographed in 1977

By 1950 the age of the carrier was nearly at an end. The more farsighted had turned to motor transport and the yard of The Plough (on the site of the Regent Arcade) and the car park in Rodney Road had largely replaced the inns as stabling points. Older readers might remember Bowles of Ford, Gilletts of Winchcombe and Perretts of Shipton Oliffe who had all been carriers before changing their cart for a motor coach. So, too, did Pulhams of Bourton on the Water, who still operate today.

I will end this brief account of Cheltenham's country carriers with an amusing reminiscence which appeared in the *Gloucestershire Echo* in March 1954 following a report of the death of one of the last carriers:

There was a Mr Swallow who lived at Guiting Power and traded between there and Cheltenham. My wife tells me she was a passenger one night with him and they simply could not get the horse or driver past Cider Jack's as it was called (opposite the Dowdeswell Reservoir). After waiting till she lost her patience, she went into the bar and told him in no uncertain manner what she thought of him, to the extent if Mr Swallow did not swallow what was left mighty quick she was heading back to Cheltenham!

After all this, she would have been lucky if she wasn't asked to get out and walk up Dowdeswell Hill or even help to push the cart.

When trams ran up Cleve Hill

In 2018 the county council carried out slip stabilisation on the B4632 on Cleve Hill. If you were caught in a queue at the end of the first week in September, you might just have noticed something remarkable - a short stretch of tram track, complete with sleepers. Yes, trams once travelled up Cleve Hill. This is the story.

The remains of the tram track with its stone sleepers excavated in September 2018

AS CHELTENHAM GREW in the second half of the 19th century, the town council began to consider providing some sort of public transport, but when trams were first suggested in 1879 they were rejected in favour of buses. Yet nothing happened for another ten years when an hourly bus service began from Lansdown Castle, at the junction of Lansdown Road and Gloucester Road, to Southam through Prestbury. These were horse-drawn, but in 1895 the council built an electricity generating station, now the Strozzi Palace, in Clarence Street and the possibility of introducing the new-fangled electric tram became real. Enter Thomas Nevins, an Irish-American entrepreneur, who in 1898 set up the Cheltenham and District Light Railway Company. He had the idea of using the electricity to power the trams. The town council was enthusiastic but why should Cleeve Hill ever be considered a destination, being such a long way out of town and approached up a steep slope? On the one hand the area was rapidly developing as an affluent outer suburb and on the other hand it had become a valuable recreational area for all Cheltonians (of course, the two functions were not always compatible). As one councillor rather optimistically forecast in 1896, "Cleeve Hill should be to Cheltenham what Clifton is to Bristol".

A route was laid out from Lansdown Castle, past Cheltenham's two railway stations, at Lansdown (the present station) and St James (opposite St Gregory's church) to Cleeve Hill. There was even talk of taking the trams to Winchcombe but knowledge that the Great Western Railway was planning a railway to the town meant that never happened.

Cleeve Hill terminus outside the Malvern View. Note the cart waiting to take goods from the tram to the inhabitants

The necessary act of parliament laid down the gauge as a narrow three feet six inches with no more than eleven inches overhanging each side of the tram. The maximum speed would be 8mph. If this seems very slow, the alternatives still depended on horsepower. The three and a half miles from Prestbury to the Malvern View Hotel on Cleeve Hill, cost £36,000 to build. Work began in February 1901 and by the end of April over five miles of track had been laid. This was quick work, no doubt the result of employing 120 labourers, many said to have followed Thomas Nevins from the USA, from where the first tramcars were imported.

All was set for a grand opening in July 1901, but tragedy struck when a tramcar on a test run only reached the Rising Sun Hotel before it began to slip back with its brakes locked on, reaching 40mph before overturning in Southam, killing two workmen. This meant that when the service did start on 17th August no passenger was allowed on the

Southam tram stop with a small waiting shelter where passengers changed trams

top deck. When two single deck tramcars arrived, built in Gloucester, all passengers for the hill had to change in Southam. The trams were immediately popular although the report in the *Cheltenham Examiner* that 10,000 travelled on the first day needs to be taken with a pinch of salt.

The affluent Cheltenham middle classes now found themselves surrounded by hundreds, if not thousands, of the very townspeople they were trying to avoid by living on the hill. In a satirical letter to the *Cheltenham Chronicle* in July 1901 a fictitious Selina Jenkins summed up this impact on the hill:

> Every little shed and shanty has invested in a pennyworth of cardboard, on which the classic legends 'Tea and Hot Water', 'Aerated Waters', 'Furnished Apartments' and so forth are inscribed in faithful and wonderful characters to entice the simple trammist.

Already an established hostelry, the profits of the Rising Sun Hotel ('newly built' in 1829) must have soared as trammists flocked through its door, but if they were of a teetotal persuasion, then across the road the

The Cleeve Hill café. The Rising Sun Hotel can just be seen on the left hand edge of the photograph

Cleeve Hill Café beckoned. In 1901, in a far-sighted speculative venture, C.J. Davies, a grocer from Suffolk Road in Cheltenham, bought a plot of land for £200 and built a rustic-looking café with a terraced pleasure garden below. Ten years later the proprietor Ernest Batstone, a pastry cook of Upper Bath Road was boasting 'Parties of 200 catered for at a moment's notice'. I doubt that would meet the requirements of trades descriptions today. Sadly the café suffered a disastrous fire in the early 1930s and the site is unrecognisable today.

Golfers, of course, could find refreshment in one of the two club houses; the Town Club, for traders and merchants, at the clubhouse on the main road, now 1 and 2 Cleeve Hill, or in the pavilion of the Cheltenham Golf Club for gentlemen, bordering the common near the Malvern View,

The Malvern View Hotel Tea Garden can be seen in this postcard. The clubhouse of the Cheltenham Golf Club stands on the far left and golfers can be seen in the foreground on the first tee

now Stonefields House. The Malvern View, then a small hotel, set up its own tea garden as shown in the postcards designed for the visitors to send home to extol the delights of the hill. From the tram terminus outside the Malvern View the trammist had to walk a hundred yards or so further on to sample the delights of the Geisha Tea House - a little bit of Japan recreated on the Cotswold scarp. In 1911 Annie Smith from Cheltenham was the proprietor, helped by Fanny Yiend who lived on the hill. Annie provided weekend accommodation from Saturday evening to Monday morning for 10/6d (52p). Sadly this too no longer exists, demolished in 1988 as rot and woodworm had rendered it beyond restoration. However a faint echo of its architectural style survives in the first floor balcony of

The Geisha Tea House

the Cleeve Hill Hotel, built next door in 1920. And finally, across the road from the Geisha Tea House was Mrs Hobley's Cosy Corner Tea Garden. Little is known of this venture except Arthur Hobley worked as the golf professional at the Cheltenham Golf Club from 1896 to 1933.

This card was posted in 1926

With this choice of opportunities for the trammists to take refreshment and enjoy the views from Cleeve Hill, many never ventured onto the common. A few enterprising business people, mostly from Cheltenham must have made a good profit from their fellow townspeople seeking a pleasant trip out. Perhaps those who lived on the hill were not so welcoming, for they complained about the litter of discarded tram tickets, orange peel and ginger pop bottles. However no tram tickets were dropped after 1930, when the tram was replaced by the bus. The turning circle built for the bus near the top of Stockwell Lane still exists.

Although it disappeared ninety years ago the tram set the trend and Cleeve Hill continues to be a popular place today to live, for walkers, day trippers and holiday makers. To local people the common was a godsend during the covid epidemic of 2020-22. As the epidemic waned the number of visitors doubled from pre-pandemic levels, but today's visitors are more likely to come by car.

Local bus services nearly 70 years ago

This article on transport considered some of the local bus services which replaced the carriers' carts. It is based on a guide I have acquired which is dated 1958. It makes fascinating reading and will, no doubt, bring back memories for older readers.

B Y 1958 BUS services were much more used than the trains, for they were more accessible and frequent with both Bishop's Cleeve and Winchcombe being served by three different companies. Yet not a single company operating in 1960 is operating today; victims of increasing car ownership and rationalisation of services.

Some people in Bishop's Cleeve will remember the demolition of the shelter and public convenience, built to celebrate the coronation of Queen Elizabeth II in 1953, when the entrance to Tesco was built in 1998. It was the main bus stop in Bishop's Cleeve. Twelve times on a weekday and four times on a Sunday, villagers could wait there to join a service to the Royal Well bus station in Cheltenham from Evesham via Kemerton, provided jointly by the Bristol Omnibus and Stratford Blue companies. The Bristol company provided most of the services around

A Bristol Omnibus service for Smiths' workers at The Grange in Bishop's Cleeve in 1976 (W.Potter)

Cheltenham, including two services from that town to Tewkesbury through Bishop's Cleeve: Service 62 ran generally hourly via Aston Cross and Service 62A ran through Stoke Orchard. There were no services on Sunday mornings. In total villagers had a choice from 33 weekday departures to Tewkesbury, which contrasts starkly with the Stagecoach T hourly service today.

Woodmancote was served by Kearsey's Service 14 from Cheltenham to Gotherington and on to Alderton, Great Washbourne and Stanway, although all except two terminated in Gotherington. Timings were anything but regular. Four services left Gotherington for Royal Well between 8am and 9.30am on a weekday, but then there was an hour's wait. Coming back from Cheltenham, miss the 6pm service, the next one left at 7.30pm with the next, and last, at 10.15pm, which was usually before the cinemas finished showing their films. In Kearsey's timetables 'Bishop's Cleeve' was the stop between Gotherington and Woodmancote. After the latter stop the buses went down Two Hedges Road and stopped at The Green in Bishop's Cleeve, always referred to as 'Cleeve Estate'.

The main bus stop in Winchcombe is still found in Abbey Terrace. Cheltenham services were much more limited than Bishop's Cleeve's.

An elderly Kearsey double-decker bus formed the 8.25am from Woodmancote to Cheltenham in early 1965

Bristol Omnibus provided seven services during the week and four on a Sunday to Cheltenham, with two extended the other way to Broadway. Readers might remember Gillett's coaches. Confusingly the company

A 1960 advertisement for Gillett's coaches

operated a different number of services at different times on different days of the week; three on Monday, Tuesday, Friday and Sunday; four on Wednesday and Thursday with five on Saturday. Also Kearsey's Service 16 had a similar pattern, although its buses did not run until lunchtime and none at all ran on a Wednesday. Sixteen departures for Cheltenham on a Saturday provided the most frequent service from Winchcombe. All the buses stopped on Cleeve Hill, where the remains of a Cheltenham electric tramcar provided a welcome waiting shelter for the passengers.

Until 1970 the body of tramcar No.13 formed the bus shelter on Cleeve Hill

This also marked the turning circle for Cheltenham's town Service 1, which had replaced the trams when they were withdrawn in March 1930 and which provided a frequent half hourly service to the centre and the two railway stations. Despite the increase in car ownership both Bishop's Cleeve and Winchcombe enjoy regular bus services to Cheltenham, but the variety of other destinations has shrunk compared to services nearly seventy years ago.

The Honeybourne Railway Line 1906-2018

I wrote several articles on the Cheltenham to Honeybourne railway line for the Directory, starting with the story behind the first trains to link Broadway and Winchcombe through Gretton and Gotherington and Bishop's Cleeve to Cheltenham and ending with the completion of the steam heritage railway's line to Broadway in 2018.

B Y THE END of the 19th century the Great Western Railway had the unenviable nickname of the 'Great Way Round' and a direct line between Birmingham and Bristol was seen as one of the essential routes to erase this unwanted label. Not only would it compete with the Midland Railway's route (which still exists) but would prevent other companies from building in the area; as far back as 1860 there had been a plan to link Winchcombe to Beckford. So an act of parliament was passed in 1899 and building

UP TO DATE !

CHELTONIA—Pullman return to Winchcombe, please
[SKETCH BY OUR ARTIST—N... 151]

began in November 1902 from Honeybourne. Originally it had been planned to start from Cheltenham, but the council had objected to some of the proposals and this delayed the work there. The navvies who built the line lived in camps which followed the construction. The flat area, now planted with saplings, at the western entrance to the Greet tunnel was the site of one of the camps. At Gotherington the logbook for the school recorded twenty three railway children attending in November 1905, but by the time the school had been extended fifteen months later, only two navvy families remained.

Although a route for express trains, costs were kept down as much as possible. The original survey included a four mile tunnel under Cleeve Hill with the line passing between Winchcombe and Sudeley, giving the townspeople a much more convenient station than that at Greet. The actual line deviated from this route at the Chicken Curve

The collapsed viaduct at Stanway

embankment, the site of a major landslip in January 2011 which closed the line for over eighteen months and cost almost a million pounds to repair. Embankments were built largely from spoil from the cuttings, but their foundations and drainage caused concerns for the Great Western Railway and British Railways until the line's closure in 1976. During the construction, in November 1903 a major disaster occurred when part of the Stanway viaduct collapsed, killing four workmen.

The line was opened in stages from Honeybourne where it met the Oxford to Worcester line; to Broadway in August 1904, to Toddington in December 1904 and to Winchcombe in February 1905. The tunnel at Greet delayed the opening of the next stage and so passengers were carried by motor bus, starting from The George Hotel in the town to the station, then through Gretton, Gotherington and Bishop's Cleeve

" Winchcombe's First Motor Bus." starting for maiden trip Feb. 18. 1905. Station in background.

Photo J. P. Hawley, Chemist, Winchcombe.

to Cheltenham. This journey took eighty minutes and the bus ran three return services each weekday and so for the first time local people could travel to Cheltenham by public transport. When the railway reached Bishop's Cleeve in June 1906, the bus started from there, but from 1 August the trains ran all the way into St James' station in Cheltenham.

St James station in St James Square shortly before closure in 1966

The timetable then showed eight trains a day linking the stations along the line to Cheltenham.

I then delved into the archives to discover an account in the Cheltenham Chronicle of the opening of the line into Cheltenham on 1st August 1906.

It ran: '8.05am and 8.51am ought to be figures easily remembered in connection with the full opening of the Honeybourne branch, for they are the times in the morning at which the first train ran out of St James'-square Cheltenham, and of the one that came into it. Precisely to time, rail motor-car No.69, with trailer No.6, departed without any ceremony. There were six passengers – three for Bishop's Cleeve, two for Gotherington, and one for Winchcombe. The first train in, No.65 car,

Opening day at Winchcombe station

with No.24 trailer, brought in a goodly freight of 51 passengers, about a dozen of whom came from Evesham, and all were through bookings. It was found that one lady who wanted to go to Birmingham had got into this car by mistake, and was sent back by the next car to Honeybourne for her connecting train. It is interesting to note that Mr R.E. Steel, solicitor of Cheltenham, who was one of the first passengers by the in-train, was also a first passenger from Cheltenham when the Banbury line was opened [1881], and through the Seven Tunnel [1886]. The bookings by the second out-train, at 10:01am, numbered 18, Bishop's Cleeve taking three, Bretforton one, Campden two, Gotherington three, Honeybourne six, Stratford one, and Winchcombe two.

Two rail motors will for the present work the traffic. The one, starting from Cheltenham at 8.05am will run via Honeybourne to Moreton in Marsh and return and do a journey to and from Evesham and finish up with a return one to Honeybourne, ending at Cheltenham at 7.18pm. The other car will run chiefly between Evesham and Cheltenham, via Honeybourne, doing four journeys, the first being at 7.33am and the fourth ending at 9.51pm. There will be two goods trains each way between Honeybourne and Gloucester. From four to four and a half hours are allowed for each journey (of the goods train), including calls and stops at the several stations.'

Interestingly none of these early passengers either came from or travelled to Broadway, the terminus of the heritage railway. But the *Gloucester Citizen* showed itself already to be alive to the tourist potential. On the opening of the line it commented: 'The new line passes

At opening Broadway station was still not completed, hence the piles of sand on the platform (I.Crowder)

through a district rich in picturesque scenery and historic interest. The pretty village of Broadway affords many pleasant examples of stone-built houses with quaint decorative qualities.' Today people can again travel to Broadway by train to enjoy the 'picturesque scenery' and the 'pretty village'.

Incidentally, the expresses for which the line had been built, did not start for another two years, after another new line was built between Birmingham and Stratford on Avon. The remains of Cheltenham's new station on that line at Malvern Road can still be seen along the Honeybourne cycle path.

How many people today realise that until March 1960 it was possible to travel by train between Bishop's Cleeve and Winchcombe? The journey might have taken just eleven minutes, including a stop at Gretton, but on a weekday there were only five trains and on Sundays

Bishop's Cleeve station on the last day of the local train service, 5 March 1960 (W.Potter)

there were none. For Cheltenham workers and schoolchildren the trains were very convenient, as they ended at St James' station opposite St Gregory's church, but miss the 7.45am train at Bishop's Cleeve for

Winchcombe and you had to wait until 2.42pm for the next one. Miss the 10.17am at Winchcombe and the next train to Bishop's Cleeve came at 6.35pm! On Saturdays two shoppers' trains filled those gaps.

The line was one of the last main lines to be built by the Great Western Railway but even before its fiftieth birthday it was in decline. Bishop's Cleeve station lost its staff in 1950 and Gotherington was closed completely in 1955, although the buildings survive today in private hands and provide a highlight of the modern train journey. The

The Cornishman at Bishop's Cleeve c.1958 (T.Curr)

local stopping passenger trains were withdrawn in March 1960 and the goods yard at Bishop's Cleeve three years later. Winchcombe goods yard remained open until 1964 as did that at Broadway. The original station and signal box at Winchcombe were demolished within a year, leaving only the goods shed, now the home of the heritage railway's carriage and wagon works. The present signal box at Winchcombe came from Hall Green near Birmingham. Broadway's goods shed is now part of the caravan site on the opposite side of the road to the station. By the end of 1965 Bishop's Cleeve's attractive Cotswold stone signal box had gone and so only the station master's house and a pair of railwaymen's semis on Station Road serve as reminders of the site of the railway station. At Toddington the goods yard lasted until January 1967 after which it was used to store wagons and the goods shed itself survives in use by the heritage railway.

However these local Cheltenham to Honeybourne passenger and goods services amounted to only a small proportion of the traffic on the line. From 1957 to 1962 a handful of long distance diesel trains ran daily between the West Midlands and South Wales. Some readers might remember the crack express *The Cornishman* which ran between Wolverhampton and Penzance from 1952 to 1962, when it was diverted on to the line which runs through Cheltenham's existing station. Until 1966 summer Saturday trains starting from Wolverhampton transported holidaymakers to places like Paignton and Ilfracombe, but from 1966 the only regular passenger service remaining was the twice daily bubblecar

A Wolverhampton to West Country Saturday holiday train hauled by 7001 Sir James Milne at Bishop's Cleeve in July 1963 (W.Potter)

The last Gloucester to Leamington train passing through Toddington on 23 March 1968 (T.Curr)

Winchcombe station and goods yard became the centre for reclaiming the rails, October 1979

between Gloucester and Leamington Spa, which ran, often empty, until March 1968. The racecourse station, opened in 1912, also closed for the special trains carrying the race goers at the same time but was re-opened in 1972 until the closure of the line in 1976.

We can too easily forget today just how much freight went by rail in the 1960s and 1970s and so the line continued to be used by goods trains after the regular passenger trains ceased to use it. In 1972 twenty trains a day were passing along the line and it was the derailment of coal wagons near Winchcombe on 25th August 1976 which brought about closure. British Rail estimated the cost of restoring the line to be almost the same as the value of the metal rails themselves and so the track was removed. It had all been lifted by March 1981 when a group of enthusiasts took a lease on the old goods yard at Toddington.

In a further article I recounted the achievements of the group of enthusiasts to create the Gloucestershire Warwickshire Steam Railway. This is their story.

The death knell for the Cheltenham to Honeybourne railway line had sounded even before March 1968 when that last regular passenger service was withdrawn. After that date only goods trains and the occasional passenger train, diverted from the main Bristol to Birmingham line, travelled along the line. Its end, however, dragged on, despite the obvious fact that British Rail was losing money keeping it open for the few trains which used it. Matters nearly came to a head in June 1972 when they announced the line would be closed on 1st January 1974. This news got Cheltenham councillors very excited and they spent £60,000 on a report into the feasibility of building a north to south relief road on the abandoned track. Imagine their dismay when less than a year later British Rail changed its mind. Trains continued to run.

The eventual closure came unexpectedly with that derailment in August 1976 of the coal wagons at Chicken Curve to the east of the site of Winchcombe station. After much deliberation and delay British Rail decided not to repair the damage and so the track and land was offered to an embryonic Gloucestershire Warwickshire Steam Railway Society. This had been started by just four visionaries who had held a public meeting in Willersey in 1976 with the intention of keeping the line intact. Not surprisingly this small society could not afford the purchase, and it was ironical that three years later in July 1979 when funds had been promised, British Rail changed its mind for a second time, declaring it wanted to keep the route open, despite having already removed the rails. Then in August just a year later British Rail changed its mind for a third time. Its chairman Sir Peter Parker announced it was prepared to sell the line because of the financial problems it was facing. The society immediately started negotiations with a view to initially reopening the stretch from Toddington to Honeybourne. There was great enthusiasm for the project with over 700 people attending a meeting in Shaftesbury Hall in the centre of Cheltenham in February 1981 when the society first appealed for volunteers. Tim Bazeley, the secretary, painted for the audience an ambitious future as a tourist and community railway possessing thirty five steam locomotives. In this respect subsequent events indicated that enthusiasm outran reality.

However there was enough enthusiasm to ensure wheels began to turn the very next month. A company was set up to raise capital for the purchase, and both the company and its supporters still continue to manage their developments and finances carefully and prudently to

Tim Bazeley waving from the first locomotive driven along the short re-laid track at Toddington in June 1981

ensure the continuing success of the railway. In March the Toddington site was leased from British Rail so that a start could be made before the actual purchase. It was to become the centre of the heritage railway's operations. By early June one hundred and twenty yards of track had been laid towards Winchcombe (not Honeybourne as originally planned) and by late June in an act of faith, steam locomotive 2807 had arrived from the famous locomotive scrapyard at Barry for restoration. It took twenty nine years to restore to working condition but it still runs on the railway today.

The first public train ran over 700 yards of track towards Didbrook on 22nd April 1984. The next year Didbrook had been reached and the year following the site of the future Hayles Abbey Halt. On 8th

A train to Didbrook in June 1986

March 1987 the first passenger train steamed into Winchcombe station which was still in the process of being rebuilt out of a station building from Monmouth. Gretton was reached in 1990, Far Stanley in 1995 and Gotherington in 1997. Here a new platform had to be built as the original station lay in private hands. It was an important day on 7th April 2003 as HRH the Princess Royal declared the southern terminus at Cheltenham Racecourse open.

Work then started on the northern stretch of the line. Track was laid across Stanway viaduct in 2005, to Laverton in 2011 and Little

Buckland in 2017. During this year the rebuilt Hayles Abbey Halt was opened. By that date the completely new station at Broadway was well on the way to completion and the first trains arrived on Good Friday, 30th March 2018. The result of all this activity is that the Gloucestershire Warwickshire Steam Railway is now one of the longest heritage lines in the country providing a 28 mile round trip. If you haven't already travelled along it, it is well worth a visit.

Broadway station being rebuilt in 2017

EVENTS

Christmas Feasting Medieval Style

In 1289 Richard Swinfield, Bishop of Hereford, spent Christmas at his manor house in Prestbury. A surviving record provides a fascinating insight into the extravagant celebrations of a medieval bishop.

PRESTBURY HAD BELONGED to the Bishops of Hereford since long before 1066. They had built a manor house which provided a convenient resting place on the journey from Hereford to London, where the bishop sat in the House of Lords. Remains of the moat which surrounded it can still be seen next to the race course at the end of Park Lane. Adjacent to the manor house they laid out a park for hunting – hence Prestbury Park. In 1249 Bishop Peter of Savoy even gained a royal charter to create a market town to compete with nearby Cheltenham, but it failed, leaving only the name *The Burgage* (i.e. a rental property in a town) to remind us of an ill-fated venture.

So it was here that Bishop Swinfield with his entourage decided to spend Christmas 1289, breaking his journey to London. His chaplain, John of Kempsey, kept a meticulous record of the expenditure and from it we can learn much about the bishop's Christmas.

Preparations had begun in early November when one of the servants, Robert of Callow, was sent to prepare charcoal for the fires and brew the

Bishop Richard from his tomb

ale, which at that time lacked hops and soon went off. We also know from excavations carried out in 1951 that new chimneys were probably built in the kitchen and an oven repaired. Also a covered walkway was constructed from the kitchen to the hall to keep the food warm. Richard and his entourage arrived on 22nd December, having taken five days for the journey from his manor house at Bosbury, near Ledbury, such was the state of the roads in what was a very wet December.

A representation of a medieval feast

Christmas Eve was a time of abstinence and so the bishop dined only on fish – herrings, codling, conger eels and salmon. On Christmas Day the feasting probably began about noon. For this John of Kempsey recorded the purchase of a boar, which was then roasted, two and a half carcasses of beef, two calves, four does, four pigs, sixty fowl, eight partridges, two geese and 900 eggs, accompanied by bread and butter and cheese and washed down with over seventy pints of wine and untold quantities of the ale prepared by Robert of Callow. To modern minds there was clearly an overload of protein, but whether this was because fruit and vegetables had been grown on the bishop's estate and not bought and so not appearing in the accounts, or whether they were regarded as food only for the poor, we shall never know. This food was probably shared by about fifty men (no ladies then) and we can imagine a crowded hall, with the hustle and bustle of the servants, the noise, the mingled smells of food, candles and humans, with the dogs rooting in the rushes on the floor for scraps from the tables.

Such a meal must have competed with the main event of the day; a mass to celebrate Christ's birth. We know this took place, as 4s 1d (20p) was collected for the poor – rather less than the 5s 8d (27p) spent on the salmon for Christmas Eve. The festivities continued for another two days and Richard managed to fit in hunting for deer in the park, but then he had to set out for London, where he arrived on 7th January. He never liked staying in London and so it is no surprise that he was back in Prestbury for a month's stay by 25th January. Richard remained bishop until 1316 and continued to visit Prestbury, but never again do the records provide such detail of a medieval Christmas feast.

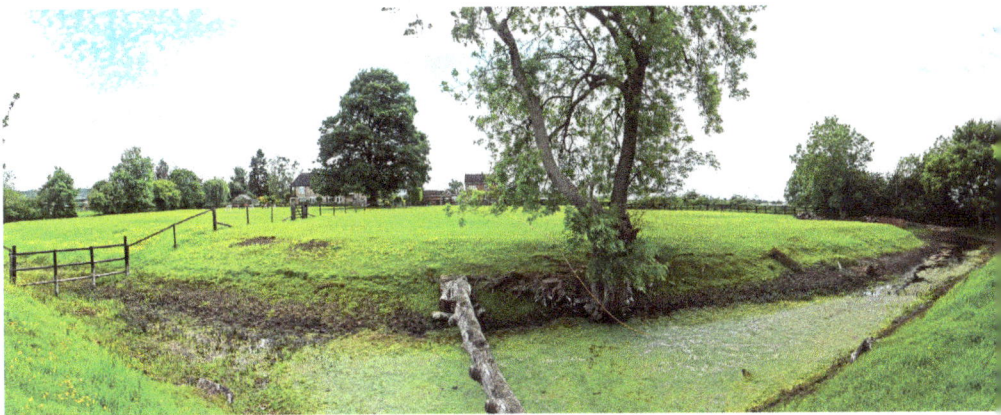

Only part of the moat of the Prestbury manor house still survives

Cheltenham Races in 1820 and 1855

I wrote several articles with a horse-racing theme for the Directory to coincide with Cheltenham's Gold Cup meetings in March. Here are accounts of the race meetings in 1820 and 1855.

THE 1820 MEETING was one of the very first meetings in Cheltenham's history, for the races had only really started in 1818, as part of the spa season from April to November. At that time races were held over a figure-of-eight course high up on Cleeve Common – not an easy place to reach in the days of horses and carriages. For three days at the end of July they provided an addition to the attractions designed to keep the idle rich busy in 'The Merriest Sick Resort on Earth'. So much is known about the 1820 meeting because it formed the subject of a ballad 'Cheltenham Races: A Poetical Description' which was sold around the town for the

The racecourse shown on an early Ordnance Survey map

considerable sum of two shillings. Although chiefly attacking some of the personalities in town, the ballad also successfully captures the race atmosphere.

Racing sat badly with the ancient uses of the common as pasture for the local villagers' animals. The anonymous writer of the ballad didn't disguise his disdain:

With sluggish step departs the surly clown,
And drives his flock from Cleeve's deserted down.

CHELTENHAM RACES,

A newspaper advertisement for the races

The author's interest lay in poking fun at the fashionable visitors to the spa. Early in the ballad he contrasted them with the rustic race-goers from Winchcombe; again his disdain for those not of the beau-monde is made clear:

In Winchcombe's streets the heavy laden car
With ill-greased wheels is heard to groan from far:
The horrid oath, the whip's loud sounding crack,
The merry laugh of boy on donkey's back, ...
Up Postlip bank winds slow the rustic throng,
And clouds of dust attend their march along;
But not such clouds as Southam's hill can boast,
Where Cheltenham's varied, gay, unnumbered host
Roll, like the stormy waves on Brighton's shore,
And as they rise condense yet more and more.....
When first these steeds were harness'd for the day,
With all the colours of the rainbow gay
They shone transplendent. Chestnut, bay and black
Now seem as tho' they travell'd with a sack
Of wheaten flour from Cheltenham's lower mill,
And burst it as they toil'd up Southam hill.

But in other years the visitors complained of the quagmires of mud on the unmade tracks leading up the hill.

Having reached the common, the carriages were drawn up to form a figure of eight course near the present pylons. The races, however, formed only part of the days' attractions, as the ballad continues:

Why should I sing of stalls with canvas spread
O'er glittering toys, and dolls, and gingerbread,
While statelier booths erect their heads on high,
And throw their baits to every passer by?
Here tight-rope dancers with their active spring
Disgrace on Richter, and on Sanchi bring;
One shilling shows you, all as large as life,
The lion, tiger, keeper, and his wife;
And Gloucester heroes teach for twice nine pence
The science elegant of self-defence;
With thousand other idle schemes to drain
The hard-earn'd savings of each rustic swain.

In 1842 the grandstand which had been built in 1835 was demolished. Starting in 2023 members of Gloucestershire Archaeology have been investigating the site near the pylons. In 2024 they unearthed the foundations of the south-east corner

What a sight it must have been on this windswept upland! No doubt some of the 'rustic swains' tried to recover their losses by joining gangs of pickpockets who were skilled in stripping the carriages of their valuables whilst the occupants' attention was elsewhere on the races. Such was the fear of the less-desirable features which accompanied the races that there soon developed a backlash led by the outspoken Reverend Francis Close ('The Pope of Cheltenham'), who moved to the town in 1824, but that story appears here in another article.

The races on Cleeve Hill came to an end in 1842 when they were replaced by a Grand Annual Steeplechase held in the spring at various locations around the town, including Prestbury Park. This formed part of the Rosehill estate which was bought in 1853 by Charles Dodson. He was obviously no such race goer, for in January 1855 he banned all racing on his land. What a disaster for the racing community. But it responded swiftly and planned to return to Cleeve Hill, with the memory of well-contested races across the open downland of the common. Thus was held a long-forgotten meeting. Dates were fixed for Thursday and Friday 28th and 29th June and subscription lists were opened, principally to make the prize money worthwhile. The committee needed prestigious patrons and the Duke of Beaufort and Captain Francis Berkeley were invited to be the stewards. £20 was paid to the freeholders of Bishop's Cleeve for the privilege of racing on their common land. But what of the races themselves? Five were planned each day, with the

Captain Berkeley

most valuable Gloucestershire Stakes on Thursday and the Cheltenham Handicap on Friday being the main contests.

The scenes on the hill must have brought the memories flooding back as a temporary grandstand, booths, sideshows, refreshment tents and stalls were set up, but there was also a modern twist; the Great

GREAT WESTERN RAILWAY.
Cheltenham Races.

ON THURSDAY and FRIDAY, the 28th and 29th June, 1855, a SPECIAL TRAIN will leave Swindon at 9.30 a.m. for Cheltenham, calling at

Purton	...	...	...	...	at	9.38
Minety	...	...	...	...	,,	9.45
Cirencester	...	...	...	...	,,	9.45
Tetbury	...	...	...	...	,,	10. 0
Brimscomb	...	...	...	...	,,	10.18
Stroud	...	...	...	...	,,	10.25
Stonehouse	...	...	...	. .	,,	10.35

And will return from Cheltenham each Evening at Eight o'clock.. FARES.

SINGLE FARE for the DOUBLE JOURNEY.
No Luggage allowed.

The Tickets issued on Thursday will not be available for the return Journey on Friday.

For the accommodation of Passengers from Bath, and the Wilts and Somerset Line, this Train will await the arrival of the Up Express at Swindon.

June 20th, 1855.

The first recorded railway race special

Western Railway organised a race special from Swindon to Cheltenham. This must have been the very first race special ever run to Cheltenham although, unlike today, the punters had to make their own way from the station in St James' Square to the top of Cleeve Hill. Carriages went the long way round along the London road and through Whittington, but for those who could not afford them, the same long dusty climb through Prestbury had not changed. Enterprising inhabitants in Prestbury set up beer stalls along the route to help them on their way.

'The sport was excellent,' reported the *Gloucester Journal*, but it added that the fields were thin, with only five running in the Gloucestershire Stakes. Nevertheless it was an exciting finish when Mr Gulliver's *Collingwood* at 5-2 defeated the favourite, Lord John Scott's *Le Juif*, backed at 5-4. The second day was poorly attended; the crowds were 'anything but numerous or fashionable' according to the *Gloucester Chronicle*. Neither steward turned up. Even the main race, the Cheltenham Handicap, lacked any excitement and proved to be a 'one-horse race'; Mr Powell's *Redemption* winning easily from a field of seven.

Sadly for the promoters, there was no escaping the fact that the races had been a disappointment. The glory days had not been recaptured and there was to be no repeat. So why was this? It was not just the inconvenient location. Cheltenham was no longer 'the merriest sick resort on earth', as it had become a more sober and restrained town, some would say largely from the influence of the Reverend Francis Close. In addition, steeplechasing was inherently more exciting and unpredictable than flat racing so when racing did return to Prestbury Park at the foot of Cleeve Hill some fifty years later, the course was set for steeple chasing, not flat racing

Cleeve Lodge stables were built c.1850 as the common's turf attracted trainers long after the races were no longer held on the common. Owen O'Neill was the last trainer who regularly used the hill, leaving in 2004

Christmas Day in the Workhouse

For Christmas 2011 I investigated how the paupers in Winchcombe workhouse celebrated the festival.

THE LINE 'It was Christmas Day in the workhouse' is likely to bring a smile to the lips of many readers of a certain age, for what follows can be both ribald and humorous. The words form the opening line of a sentimental poem written in 1877 by George Sims in which the fictional narrator criticises the fleeting Christmas Day bonhomie of local do-gooders, when the normal workhouse conditions had killed his wife the Christmas before. Workhouses had existed since an act of 1834 to provide a safety net for those unable to look after themselves at home, typically through old age, illness and

Winchcombe workhouse in 1951, by which time the central block had already been demolished (© Crown copyright NMR [Harold Wingham Collection])

infirmity, unemployment and as orphans and unmarried mothers. When Winchcombe's workhouse was opened in Back Lane in September 1836, its inmates came from thirty surrounding parishes stretching from Bishop's Cleeve to Temple Guiting and from Dumbleton to Hawling.

It was one of over six hundred workhouses set up by the act which had been passed to curb the large sums spent on the poor, because this had greatly alarmed ratepayers. Costs were to be cut by making the workhouse an unpleasant place where life would be even worse than that of the poorest labourer who managed to avoid it. As inmates were at least fed, clothed and housed, life had to be made worse in other ways – split families, long and tedious manual work, humiliating uniforms and a rigorously applied daily timetable. The paupers were therefore hardly likely to be allowed to celebrate Christmas - although we mustn't forget that the modern celebration of Christmas only developed after Prince Albert married Queen Victoria in 1841, seven years after the act had been passed. So how <u>were</u> Christmases celebrated in Winchcombe workhouse?

In 1847 the government first allowed guardians, who were responsible for the running of workhouses, to spend money from the rates on Christmas extras. Two years later in Winchcombe we find the eighty nine inmates "humbly begging" the guardians to "allow something extra for a Christmas dinner" and from then onwards roast beef and plum pudding became the paupers' traditional Christmas feast. As the years passed, private charity became more common and in 1901 the workhouse master and mistress, Mr and Mrs Healey, recorded the inmates' thanks to sixteen local benefactors who provided gifts and also to "the Ladies and Gentlemen who kindly assisted in entertaining the inmates on Christmas and New Year's Day". Eleanor Adlard of the family who owned Postlip Mill headed the list of benefactors with sweets, crackers, tobacco, tea, sugar and oranges. Similarly, Lady Elcho from Stanway House sent toys, tobacco, tea, sugar and sweets, whilst Miss Wedgwood, the daughter of the rector of Stanton, provided a traditional Christmas tree with candles.

Christmas 1929 was the last one in the workhouse. The forty five inmates even enjoyed prolonged entertainment with a New Year's concert followed by an individual gift. Mr Will Rose from Cheltenham put on a magic lantern show, Walter Haslam, St Peter's church organist, led community singing and four inmates put on sketches. A week into the new year Miss Adlard invited all the inmates to tea. We are now a long way from the punitive terms of the 1834 act which came to an end only four months later in April 1930. Winchcombe workhouse then became a public assistance institution and the building survived another quarter of a century before being replaced by Langley Court.

Langley Court today

Celebrating Queen Victoria's Diamond Jubilee in 1897

Queen Elizabeth II celebrated her Diamond Jubilee in June 2012. To coincide with it, I turned the clock back over a century to that other Diamond Jubilee, celebrated by Queen Victoria.

OUR VICTORIAN ANCESTORS celebrated Jubilee Day, Tuesday 22nd June 1897 with great enthusiasm. Emma Dent of Sudeley was as anxious to link her name to the Diamond Jubilee as she had been to the Golden Jubilee ten years earlier, paying for lasting memorials for Winchcombe: a refurbished church clock and the restoration of the stone cross in the churchyard. Emma was already a great patron of Winchcombe having financed the building of Dent's almshouse in Abbey Terrace in 1865 and the infants' school and school house by the church in 1867. No doubt in use for the jubilee celebrations was the open-air swimming pool on the Beesmoor Brook near the bottom

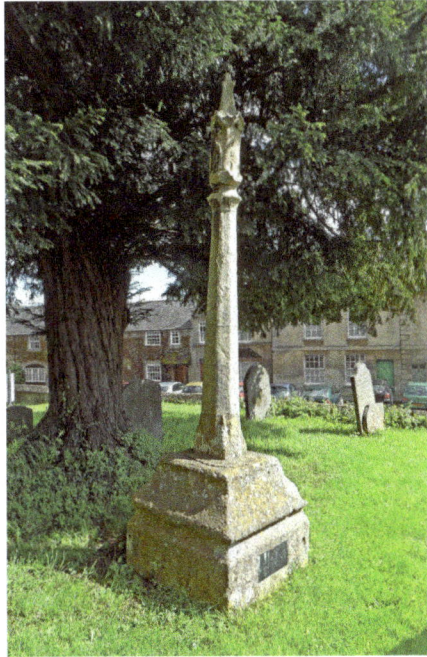

Emma Dent's restored cross still stands in St Peter's churchyard

of Castle Street, which opened in 1893 at a cost of £400, also paid for by Emma. Mike Lovatt in his book *The River Isbourne in the Service of Mankind* tells how it opened in August, although an increasingly frail Emma was too ill to attend. It remained in use for forty years until the appearance of raw sewage in the absence of any filtration forced its closure. It did, however, enjoy a brief renaissance in the early years of the Second World War when it was cleaned out by the Allied soldiers stationed at Sudeley. They built a canoe which sank almost as soon as it was launched and they never had the courage actually to swim in the pool. It then gently decayed back into nature.

Not to be outdone by Emma, the townspeople also rose to the occasion by subscribing £62 to pay for a variety of activities. Flags and bunting decorated the main streets. The Toddington Band led a procession to St Peter's church for a service of thanksgiving before the dedication of Emma Dent's gifts. Then followed a public dinner, sports and dancing with a tea provided for the children and the 'poor women' of

The swimming pool in the 1920s (Winchcombe Museum)

the town. Jubilee day concluded with large crowds making their way up Langley Hill to enjoy the town's bonfire and firework display.

In Bishop's Cleeve the celebrations extended over two days. On the Tuesday the National Anthem was sung from the church tower and a hundred villagers sat down to 'a sumptuous repast' in the orchard behind the King's Head, followed by a sixty yard race; one yard for each year of the reign. We can imagine the excitement the following day as nearly 500 schoolchildren from Cleeve and the surrounding villages, marched from the school (now St Michael's Centre) to the rectory (Cleeve Hall) behind the band of the Cheltenham Rifles, looking forward to sports and tea in the field behind the rectory. Grown ups were not forgotten - more races, a cricket match and boating on the rectory lake, since filled in. After tea each child received some sweets and a Jubilee mug before the celebrations came to an end when fire balloons were released into the night sky.

There were more fun and games on the top of Cleeve Hill. Local people and the Conservators of the common had worked for nearly a week to build a forty foot high bonfire out of wood and gorse, coal and tar barrels, but disaster struck when it 'was prematurely fired by some evil-disposed person' and reduced to ashes. Despite a reward of £10 the culprit(s) were never caught. Undaunted, Heming Shipway, chairman of the parish council, rounded up sixty schoolchildren from the village to carry faggots of wood up the hill to rebuild it. Others joined in and by Jubilee night a sixty foot high replacement was ready. At the appointed time of 10pm, Arthur Griffiths of The Grange in Bishop's Cleeve climbed the wooden ladder to set it alight. The beacon on Cleeve Hill achieved national fame as being the only one of the 2548 beacons to have been 'maliciously set off prematurely'.

The second beacon built on Cleeve Hill. The gentleman in the boater was probably Arthur Griffiths who later climbed the ladder to set the beacon alight (T.Curr)

Day Trip 1900 style

Many readers will have taken a day trip to our nearest seaside resort – Weston super Mare. I doubt any of them can compare to the one enjoyed by members of St Michael's church choir ('with others') from Bishop's Cleeve in July 1900 as described in the church magazine.

Choir Outing

On Monday, July 9th, our yearly Summer Choir Outing took place. The Choir, with others from the Parish, left Cleeve Station at 8.10 a.m., and travelled in a saloon carriage as far as Bristol, where, after a very short wait they had to change. They arrived at Weston-Super-Mare about half-past eleven, and then spent an hour on shore before dinner, watching Punch and Judy and such other amusements as are generally to be met with at the sea-side. A substantial dinner, to which ample justice was done, was provided by Messrs G. Huntley & Co., Beach Restaurant.

Huntley's Beach Hotel and Restaurant

Birnbeck Pier

After dinner was over, the party, some on foot, some driving, wended their way to the Pier, and thence took their passage on the *Bonnie Doone* to Cardiff, where one or two set foot on Welsh ground. A fresh breeze tempered the hot sun, thus making the voyage, which lasted altogether about two hours, very pleasant indeed. The steamer called at Penarth both going and returning.

After returning from their trip to Cardiff, the tide was well up, so that the younger members of the party were able to enjoy a good paddle, while many of the others went in for rifle-shooting and switch-back rides.

At tea, which was also provided by Messrs G. Huntley & Co., Mr. Pruen put in an appearance, and was heartily welcomed by the members of his old choir, and all others who were present. When tea was finished it was time to think of going to the station for the journey home. The train started soon after seven, and Cleeve was reached punctually at 10 o'clock. Our thanks are due to Mr. Oldacre for having again so kindly provided the means of conveyance to and from the station. We wish also to express our gratitude to those who so very liberally subscribed to the excursion.

Cleeve station stood where the road to Stoke Orchard crosses the railway bridge. It was never very convenient for the village and it closed as long ago as 1950. The party was carried there in Walter Oldacre's cart or carts. Walter was a corn merchant who at the time was building up his business in Bishop's Cleeve, which closed in 1996 and became the site for Tesco. He also carried coal in his carts from the station to drive his steam engine. It is hoped the carts had been given a good clean for the occasion.

The Beach Hotel building, now apartments, still exists in Weston, opposite the Grand Pier. It is quite a long way to Birnbeck Pier where the steamer was boarded. Plans were being made in 2019 when I wrote

The paddle steamer Bonnie Doone

the original article to restore it from its derelict state but only during the writing of this book was it announced that the National Heritage Lottery Fund had granted £5.5m to make this possible. The *Bonnie Doone* (nicknamed the *Bonnie Breakdown* - I wonder why?) was a paddle steamer, part of P and A Campbell's White Funnel fleet which operated in the Bristol channel from 1887 to 1979. The *Bonnie Doone* (272 tons and 220 feet [67 metres] long) had been built in Scotland in 1876 and was scrapped in 1913. The accompanying photograph indicates how popular such excursions were in 1900, despite seasickness being a common experience crossing the Bristol Channel. However, despite 'a fresh breeze', the party was able to enjoy a tea before making its way to the station for the journey home. No doubt Mr Oldacre carried many tired people back to the village at 10pm.

Christmas 1913 - Suffragette outrage!

Christmas 1913 was the last peacetime Christmas for five years. I discovered that it was anything but peaceful in Cheltenham, for the local newspapers had only one headline story – arson. I wrote the original article on the hundredth anniversary of the event. The details make interesting reading.

I N 1913 CHELTENHAM felt the effects of the Suffragettes' campaign of violence to secure votes for women when two Suffragettes attempted to burn down Alstone Lawn, a large country mansion on the edge of the town, which stood in large grounds where Gloucester Road meets Alstone Lane.

Alstone Lawn, a nineteenth-century print

What the newspaper report does not tell us is that the young women were not local as they came from Birmingham. It also doesn't mention that Alstone Lawn had stood for sale and empty since September 1911, so there was nobody at home to stop them from setting the house on fire. The swift action of the fire brigade limited the damage to a staircase and the roof above it, estimated at £400-£500. However the house was never repaired and was later demolished. Suffragette literature found in the house gave the police a clue to look for two young women smelling strongly of paraffin. They were soon arrested in the town as they made no attempt to flee the scene. Their attempt to seek publicity for their cause continued after their arrest when they refused to replace their stockings and shoes, and refused to give their names, so the newspapers called them 'Red' and 'Black'. They were later identified as Lilian Lenton and Olive Wharry, both of whom spent various times in prison on hunger strike.

It is not therefore surprising that this episode dominated Cheltenham's Christmas and it even appeared in newspapers as far away as the United States, Australia and New Zealand. There was strong

Pates Avenue was built where Alstone Lawn once stood (National Library of Scotland)

THE CHELTENHAM CHRONICLE
AND
GLO'SHIRE GRAPHIC

ART AND LITERARY SUPPLEMENT

No. 678.   Saturday, December 27, 19:3.

SERIOUS FIRE IN CHELTENHAM.
SUFFRAGETTES ARRESTED AND CHARGED WITH ARSON.

On Sunday morning, December 21st, about five o'clock, a fire was observed to break
out at Alstone Lawn, an empty mansion standing in the Gloucester-road, Cheltenham,
surrounded by some acres of its own grounds. The Fire Brigade was promptly called,
and the place was almost miraculously saved, the fire having well got hold. Two un-
known Suffragettes were arrested the same morning, and were remanded at the police-
court on Monday. Their boots and stockings, which were soaked in paraffin, were
taken from them, and they absolutely refused to put others on. Our photo shows them
being taken from the police-station to Worcester Gaol by Inspector Whyton and
Detective Towell, the foremost of whom is carrying the shoes and stockings. They refused to put up their hair, and they went barefoot to Worcester.

[Photo by Cheltenham Newspaper Co., Ltd.]

disapproval of their action, 'Imperialist' wrote to the Gloucestershire
Echo, 'The voters of Cheltenham are, and justly so, thoroughly sick
of votes for women'. Not until 1929 did women gain the same voting
rights as men some sixteen years later. Away from this excitement,
Christmas passed with all the usual trappings, as can be seen from the
advertisements in the newspaper.

Impact of the First World War on local communities

Whilst writing for the Directory we commemorated the centenary of the First World War. I wrote several articles looking back over a hundred years. The first coincided with the outbreak of the war on 4th August 1914. I was interested to find out how the news was received in our local area. It was followed by further articles considering the war's impact over the following four years.

I TURNED FIRST TO the front page of the *Gloucestershire Echo*. Did such a headline as WAR DECLARED AGAINST GERMANY leap out at the reader? No, far from it. In those days the *Echo's* front page was largely taken up with local advertisements but it did have a short article bemoaning the fact that the peace for which the British government had worked so hard 'could not be preserved', as Russia and Germany had already declared war on each other. However, the next day ENGLAND EXPECTS EVERY MAN TO DO HIS DUTY! did scream out from the front page, but this proved to be only an eye-catching advertisement for Cheltenham's gentleman's outfitters The Famous in the High Street. I did however find a reference to the declaration of war deep in the paper on page five but only in the editorial which began with the heading WAR BEGUN BETWEEN BRITAIN AND GERMANY. Looking back we might be amazed that such an important event in world history was considered in such a low key fashion. Yet we need constantly to remind ourselves that in 1914 the iconic war images of trenches, mud and death lay in the future. After this search in the *Echo* I turned to other sources to find out how the news was received in Winchcombe, Bishop's Cleeve and Woodmancote. The parish council minutes provided some clues.

A common theme did run through the deliberations of the three councils in that summer of 1914. But it was not the war, it was the need for a reliable water supply. Plans were in hand to create a reservoir at Lidcombe above Stanway to provide water for all three communities and it was in this context that I found the first reference in any of the minutes to the war, but even this did not occur until February 1915, when Winchcombe's council agreed to pay £3760 8s 10d (£3760.44p) towards this scheme 'at the end of the present war'. However the scheme was not completed until much later, in 1935, and then under the auspices of Evesham Rural District Council. Nevertheless the scheme would have been especially welcomed in Bishop's Cleeve and Woodmancote as they were poorly supplied with water issuing from the slopes of Nottingham Hill and Cleeve Hill. Friction was caused when Woodmancote parish council wanted to place a stopcock on The Green to build up pressure to better supply its own inhabitants, thus denying water to Bishop's Cleeve at certain times of the day. Bishop's Cleeve parish council would have none of it.

Readers might also be astonished that another important issue affecting Cleeve Hill and Winchcombe in 1914 concerned problems

This photograph shows age and youth at Woodmancote Green during the war. It was here the parish council wanted to place a water stop cock

The tram stop outside the Malvern View hotel where parked cars were creating such a problem during the war.

caused by motor traffic. In response to complaints from the locals, Woodmancote parish council was negotiating with the county council to prevent motor cars parking ('standing on the highway') near the Malvern View Hotel on the main road across the hill. Presumably these were the wealthy tourists who wanted to avoid taking the tram to reach the common. Down in Winchcombe the problem was speeding cars. The parish council wanted to impose a 10mph speed limit through the town on account of the danger to pedestrians and the dust from the road thrown up by vehicles. The county council turned both requests down.

Expanding Winchcombe's gaslight network, unblocking footpaths in Woodmancote and repairing damaged sewers in Bishop's Cleeve were other concerns of the parish councils. No doubt many local young men were already considering joining the armed forces, but to all intents and purposes the outbreak of the war had little immediate impact on our local communities.

The war had not been over by Christmas as everyone had expected. Instead it had developed into a stalemate in the trenches of the Western Front and by Christmas 1915 things had hardly changed at all. So what were the concerns of local people by then?

The war continued to have little impact on daily life at home and so most people would have been able to wish each other a Happy New Year in 1916. Take for example the concerns of Bishop's Cleeve parish council. At the turn of the year its main concern was to appoint 'a good man' to oversee the laying of sewers in Bishop's Cleeve, Southam and Woodmancote. Harry Goring was the lucky person to be chosen from the ten applicants. When the council was asked by the government to expand the agricultural land in the parish, the brief reply recorded in the council's minute book was that 'there was as much under cultivation as

Winchcombe, Glos.

When Tim Curr and myself compiled our volume Winchcombe Through Time in 2011, this was one of our favourite postcards. A fashionable Edwardian car and a group of people have obviously been added to an earlier scene, but without the dust. 'Improving' photographs is not confined to the digital age.

labour could be found for'. Later on in 1916 when the bloody battles of the Somme and Verdun were raging on the Western Front, the council's main concern was having to pay Bayshill Motor Works in Cheltenham £6.15s (£6.75p) to repair the village's fire engine.

Bishop's Cleeve's fire engine outside the Tithe Barn (T.Curr)

Over the hill in Winchcombe as 1915 drew to a close the parish council's minutes did, however, record that the council expressed its sympathy to its vice-chairman Albert Day, landlord of the George Inn, on the death of his son Charles in Gallipoli. Charles had emigrated to Australia in 1911 and had joined the Australian army. Later in the new year the councillors expressed concerns that the soldiers recovering from their wounds in the war hospital in the former infants' school on the corner of Vineyard Street were leaving their chairs out in Abbey Terrace creating a danger to pedestrians during the hours of darkness. Down the road in Gotherington the parish council minutes lack any reference to the war. Its main concern at the turn of the year was providing a new trough for the village pump.

Desperate for some references to the war, I then turned to the *Gloucestershire Echo*. Here at least were short reports from the various theatres of the war from around the world, but the paper overall

A wall plaque still records the wartime hospital in Winchcombe

reinforced the conclusion that life on the home front was carrying on largely as normal. The New Year's Eve ball at Cheltenham Town Hall had been a great success with four hundred people enjoying the location where 'everything and everyone was bright and gay.' The reference that 'The khaki uniform was very prominent' did, however, remind readers that there was a war in progress. Aladdin was playing to full houses at the Opera House in Regent Street and 'the crowds in the centre of Cheltenham on the last night of the old year were anything but depressed'. New Year's Day 1916 fell on a Saturday and the following Monday saw the start of Cavendish House's annual winter sale.

However, there were a few echoes of concern about the wartime situation. At Tewkesbury Abbey on New Year's Eve it was reported that the National Day of Penitence had been observed. It was also reported that the first Sunday in January had been set aside for a Day of Humble Prayer because the nation was facing 'a new year of such tense anxiety'. So perhaps it wasn't quite such a Happy New Year after all in 1916.

The Opera House in Regent Street is now the Everyman Theatre

Two years later on 1st January 1918 the editorial in the *Gloucestershire Echo* read: 'Whether 1918 will end the war is in the lap of the gods. One thing is absolutely certain: it will be a year of trial, endurance and sacrifice in which every citizen is called upon to take his or her share'. And so it turned out to be.

In 1917 German U-boats had begun a campaign against the merchant ships bringing food across the Atlantic. This led to shortages and although food rationing was not introduced until later in 1918, belts were tightening and government controls increasing. Bishop's Cleeve and Woodmancote both lay within the Winchcombe control area. The Food Control Committee oversaw the sale of meat. Cottagers must have been grateful that they were still allowed to kill their fattened pig at Christmas and sell some of its meat without the licence required by the butchers. This was not the only restriction which upset the butchers, for we find them meeting early in the new year to protest against the order limiting them to slaughtering only half the previous number of animals in order to conserve the supplies of meat. This led Eleanor Adlard of Postlip to complain that because the town butchers sold most of their meat on

Friday, they had little or nothing left to sell to the local villagers who could only come into town on Saturday. Always concerned for the local poor, Eleanor proposed setting up a soup kitchen for children along the lines of that already running in Churchdown charging 2d (1p) per head. Unfortunately I wasn't able to discover if this ever happened.

Winchcombe butchers near The Cross at the end of the 19th century

Government control was not confined to the sale of food. The production and sale of beer was closely monitored. Richard Arkell, owner of the local Donnington Brewery, went before the magistrates in Stow on 3rd January for brewing 192 barrels of beer the previous June, exceeding the permitted total of 180 barrels. He pleaded in his defence that the beer was of low gravity, brewed especially for the hay makers, but the magistrates were not impressed and fined him a total of £30.13s (£30.65p). As the profit on a barrel of beer at that time was 10s (50p), Richard could afford to pay.

Yet the concerns of daily life did not go away. The *Cheltenham Chronicle* reported that two absconders from the Hardwicke Reformatory near Gloucester burgled a house on Cleeve Hill during Christmas Eve. The

This Edwardian postcard shows that there were many large houses on Cleeve Hill which were worth burgling

court ordered them to be handed over to the Reformatory superintendent. The master of the Winchcombe workhouse in Langley Road reported that the fifty two inmates had enjoyed "one of the best (Christmas) treats that had been given". He went on to report that he had received £10 from Barnardos for taking in three boys and had sold two pigs for slaughter, which enabled him to buy three piglets for fattening.

This glimpse into wartime gives some indication of people's deprivations during the First World War although they seem as nothing compared to those of the Second World War. Yet their lives were being controlled as never before. The words of the Echo at the start of the year were to ring true.

A century later, on the 3rd September 2018 Bishop's Cleeve war memorial was re-dedicated by the Right Reverend Rachel Treweek, Bishop of Gloucester, after its restoration to its full height by the parish council. The shaft had been damaged in 1980 on being removed from its original location, where the Tesco roundabout now lies. This re-dedication led me to consider our local memorials to those who fell in the Great War.

War memorials were nothing new at the end of the Great War. Cheltenham's memorial to the Boer War stands in the Promenade and Winchcombe's fallen have their names inscribed on a wall plaque in St Peter's church. However, most war memorials we have today were erected after 1918. The Imperial War Museum in London has a database of over 77,000 memorials but nobody knows the exact figure.

The rededication of the war memorial in Bishop's Cleeve

Amazingly there were no national guidelines to assist the local committees as they prepared to commemorate their dead, which caused many confusing results. Some of the recorded names belong to men who had little link to the community where they are commemorated; some names appear on several memorials and other names were omitted, as it all depended on the wishes of their family. In Bishop's Cleeve only twenty one of the fifty five men whose names are recorded came from either the village itself or Woodmancote. Let me take, for example, Lionel Barnett whose name not only appears here but also on Cheltenham and Southam memorials and in St Luke's church in Cheltenham. He lived in Alstone in Cheltenham and his only a link with Bishop's Cleeve seems to have

The Winchcombe and Sudeley memorial cross contains 79 names, twelve of which also appear on Cheltenham memorials. It was dedicated on 4th August 1920 in the presence of General Sir Ian Hamilton, the famous Great War general who led the Gallipoli campaign in 1915. Also in this view can just be seen the Waddingham memorial fountain of 1910 which was demolished over half a century ago to make way for car parking

The ten names on John Oakey's war memorial in Gotherington can also be found on Bishop's Cleeve's war memorial. The memorial was extensively renovated in autumn 2024

Gretton's war memorial was dedicated on 20th September 1920 and all its seven names appear on the Winchcombe and Sudeley memorial

been as a member of the golf club on Cleeve Hill. On the other hand, Captain Hugh Turnbull, whose parents lived at Upper Colletts on Cleeve Hill, is commemorated only on his parents' grave in Bishop's Cleeve churchyard and on Cheltenham's war memorial.

The arrangements for the erection of the memorials also lay in the hands of the local committees. Those responsible for Winchcombe and Gretton

A rare photograph of a dedication, that of Southam and Cleeve Hill war memorial by the Reverend Nigel Morgan-Brown on 16th May 1920. Fourteen of its fifteen names are also inscribed on the Bishop's Cleeve memorial

memorials chose Boulton's of Bath Road, Cheltenham, who were the country's leading church sculptors and who, incidentally, built Neptune's Fountain in the Promenade. Gotherington employed John Oakey the well- known Winchcombe builder. Gretton's war memorial is unusual, as indicated by its inscription, for its base is that of the former village fountain. Colonel Forester of Gretton House provided it in 1883 but it fell out of use when the houses received their own water supply and so the base was re-used for the memorial. When the work of the committees was completed, they disbanded and today the memorials are usually the responsibility of the local parish council.

PEOPLE

Queen Elizabeth I slept here!

The original article was written in September 2019, one of the last before the covid epidemic closed the publication of the Directory. It was written to publicise the findings of that summer's archaeological investigation to find a banqueting hall built for the queen when she visited Sudeley Castle.

IN EARLY SUMMER 2018 DigVentures, an archaeological unit with a base in Bristol, led archaeological excavations in the grounds of Sudeley Castle. The main reason? In 1592 Queen Elizabeth I had visited Sudeley to celebrate the anniversary of the defeat of the Spanish Armada in 1588. The dig focused on a mound outside the gardens, thought to

Sudeley castle from the south-west. DigVentures excavated in the field to the right of the chapel

Further investigation showed the wall under the mound to be part of a garden wall

be the site of the banqueting hall, built for the festivities. Sadly for the archaeologists further investigations the next year discovered the site was that of a corner in a garden wall. Even by today, after annual digs, a banqueting hall has subsequently not been found, leading to the speculation it might never have existed. However, if we turn to the archives we can go a long way to discovering what happened during her three day stay.

Every summer Queen Elizabeth made 'progresses' around the southern part of Britain visiting the houses of her noblemen. Her noblemen regarded a visit as both an honour and a challenge, for she never travelled alone. She had a vast revenue of personal servants plus porters, coachmen and grooms with musicians for entertainment. Also members of her Privy Council travelled with her, usually about ten noblemen with their retinues, to advise on political matters because the work of governing the country had to go on.

Queen Elizabeth and her entourage entered the county at Down Ampney where she was welcomed by Giles Bridges, Lord Chandos, the owner of Sudeley Castle who was the county's Lord Lieutenant. Four nights were spent in Cirencester before travelling on to Sudeley, arriving on Saturday 9th September. She was greeted by an old shepherd who

left: Queen Elizabeth's visit is commemorated by this stained glass window in the castle (Sudeley   Castle) right: Lord Chandos (Sudeley Castle)

regaled her with a long speech bemoaning the impoverished state of the countryside, "These hills are for nothing but cottages and nothing we can present to your majesty but shepherds, but you fill our hearts with joy and our eyes with wonder." He concluded, "This lock of wool, Cotswold's best fruit, is a poor gift, but whiteness symbolises virginity's colour." This must have been the original 'humble' address!

Shepherds and virginity seemed to become themes for the visit. The next day the queen was presented with a long play recounting the Greek myth of Apollo and Daphne. Apollo pulled the sun across the sky and Daphne was the daughter of a river god. Apollo fell in love with Daphne but Daphne hated him. In the myth Daphne escaped by being transformed into a laurel tree. At the end of the very long presentation at Sudeley, Daphne appealed to Queen Elizabeth, "whither should Chastity fly but to the Queen of Chastity?" The queen, of course, never married.

The following day there was to be a presentation by local shepherds with the highpoint being the crowning of two of them as king and queen, but as the archive tersely records, 'the weather was so unfit.' It was cancelled and the shepherds lost a final chance to impress. Lord Chandos, however, did his best to impress with plenty of food and drink.

Despite all the pageantry and amusement, the work of the government had to go on. The Privy Council issued an order to prevent the overcrowding of London's prisoners by debtors for fear of spreading the plague. Elizabeth knighted five local gentleman including Sir John Higford from nearby Dixton. The visit itself was Lord Chandos' reward for raising a local militia to fight any invading Spanish army in 1588. This was a great honour but, in common with many hosts, the visit must have cost him the equivalent of a six figure sum in today's money. After three days at Sudeley, the Queen set off back to London by way of Oxfordshire, leaving the Sudeley household to recover and 21st century archaeologists to search for physical remains from the visit.

Improving the lives of both rich and poor? Tobacco growing 400 years ago

In 1619, just 27 years after Queen Elizabeth I visited Sudeley, Winchcombe and its surrounding area became famous, or even notorious, for the growing of tobacco. A folk memory of this eventful episode still survives in the town, but it was only in the 1970s through the research of Dr Joan Thirsk, then of Oxford University, that historians began to take an interest. Who were the individuals behind what Dr Thirsk called 'Projects for Gentlemen, Jobs for the Poor'?

TWO STRANDS CAME together to make tobacco growing an attractive proposition in the early 17th century – poverty and taxation. In 1575 when Queen Elizabeth I granted Winchcombe an annual fair, the town was described as being 'in a ruinous and decayed state'. The poor state of traditional agriculture could not keep thousands out of poverty but conversely tobacco growing and processing could give them work and provide profits for the gentry. The second factor was that King James I increased the tax on imported tobacco in 1604 by 4000%. Despite the king himself arguing strongly against tobacco smoking, it was gaining in popularity and so homegrown tobacco had an ever-expanding market.

Who were the individuals behind this tobacco project which stretched from Winchcombe to Cheltenham? Six have been identified by historians – a close-knit group related to each other in various ways. They belonged to what historians have called the parish gentry; gentlemen living comfortable lives whose influence largely only extended to their local area. The brains behind the project was a typical example. John Stratford was the namesake and youngest of five sons of John Stratford

The Stratfords' house in Farmcote

whose family house still dominates Farmcote. He had gone to London to seek his fortune in trade, but salt, soap, flax and cloth never produced the results he wanted and so when the opportunity to make a possible fortune out of tobacco arose, he seized it. In 1619 he rented land from John Lygon of Arle Court outside Cheltenham. John had been given it by his father, as his older brother William would inherit the ancestral home at Beauchamp Court, Madresfield in Worcestershire. The third

John Lygon's Arle Court, most of which was demolished in the 19th century

Thomas Loring's Haymes house which was completely demolished in the 18th century (Gloucestershire Archives [D309/P1])

entrepreneur, Thomas Loring of Haymes on the slopes of Cleeve Hill, came from an established local gentry family who had lived there since the 1400s. Interestingly Thomas had already experimented growing woad for dyeing cloth in an earlier attempt to give employment to the local poor and at the same time make money for himself.

Two more local gentry were also involved in the project. Giles Broadway of Postlip Hall was a cousin of John Stratford. His grandfather was the first member of the family to claim to belong to the gentry. Giles

Giles Broadway's Postlip Hall with the Happenstance Border Morris dancers at the annual Postlip Hall beer festival held in July

had enough money to buy the manor of Bishop's Cleeve in 1606 and also remodel Postlip Hall in 1614. In 1624 he then sold the former Bishop of Worcester's manor house, which was part of the manor of Bishop's Cleeve, for £3000 to another entrepreneur, the rector Timothy Gates,. The Gates' family home stood in East Anglia but his father was a younger

above: Cleeve Hall, bought by Timothy Gates for £3000 in 1624, since when the central frontage has been completely re-built

below: Sir John Tracy had Toddington Manor built in the 1620s. Today only the ruins of the gate house at the entrance to the courtyard survive as the rest was demolished and replaced by the present manor house which was built between 1819-35 and cost then more than £150,000

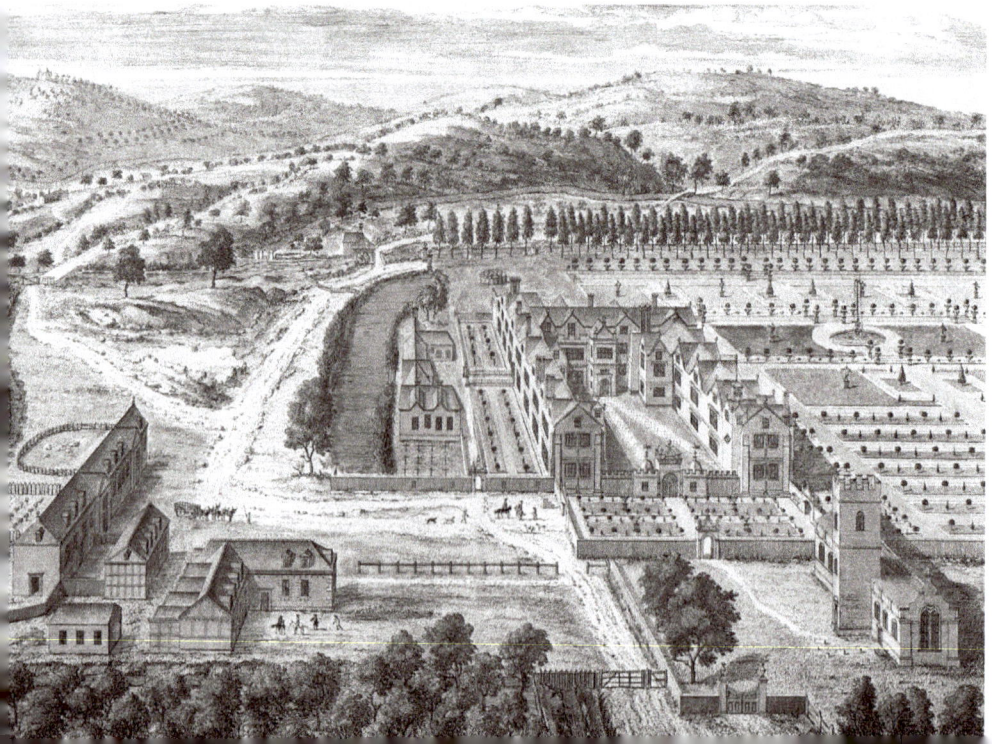

son who had moved to the Midlands. Timothy had acquired most of his fortune by marrying the widow of Peter Cox, his predecessor as rector.

Sir John Tracy of Toddington completes the list. By far the most illustrious member, his ancestor William was one of the four knights who killed Thomas à Becket in 1171. Sir John had served as a member of parliament for the county since 1597; had been high sheriff in 1609-10 and was later created a viscount in 1643. It is likely that he was invited into the venture by John Stratford, a close friend to whom he was related by marriage. However, it was John Stratford who seems to have been the chief instigator of this tobacco growing venture.

So where was the tobacco grown? I have found it very difficult to answer this question. At the time it was reported that over 100 acres (40ha) had been planted but it seems this total was made up of many small plots scattered throughout the area and I only know of a very few locations. We know that ten acres (4ha) of 'old orchard' were rented

Wickfield was the area of the ridge and furrow highlighted by melting snow in March 1976

by John Stratford from John Lygon near Arle Court from a court case when John Lygon refused to accept John Stratford's attempt to pull out of his lease when tobacco growing was declared illegal after just one harvest in 1619. Six acres were planted on Thomas Loring's Haymes estate but in very small parcels; one of which probably lay along Butts Lane in Woodmancote. Three acres were planted somewhere in Bishop's Cleeve and Giles Broadway of Postlip had five small plots. Sir John Tracy planted eight acres at Coneygree Layes, wherever that might have been. It's possible tobacco was also grown near John Stratford's house in Farmcote and in the Wickfield between Cleeve and Nottingham Hills, whilst Tobacco Close in Winchcombe could commemorate a folk memory of tobacco growing in the vicinity.

As we have seen, the motives behind the venture were to make a profit for the entrepreneurs and also give employment to the local poor. Joan Thirsk has calculated that at the busiest time of the year from May

'Tobacco barn' in the fields above Woodmancote carries a folk memory of the venture, but it is more likely to have been built for flax

to November 196 men could have been employed at 8d (3½p) per day or 262 women at 6d (2½p) per day; enough to enable every poor family in the Bishop's Cleeve and Winchcombe area to have had one member so employed. We know definitely that John Stratford paid out £1400 in labour costs - but he overstretched himself. Not enough of the tobacco was sold for a good profit and he found himself in deep financial trouble. It was said he had borrowed £5000 to finance his venture but had to sell £6000 worth of tobacco in Holland and Ireland at a considerable loss. This is the reason he tried to cancel his lease on John Lygon's land at Arle Court. The lack of clear profit and crucially the government's ban on growing tobacco at the end of the first season in 1619 led these entrepreneurs to abandon the venture. Members of the Tracy family emigrated to Virginia in North America to continue tobacco growing. John Stratford turned to flax growing to pay off his debts.

However tobacco growing was not abandoned completely as it was taken up by local people, even though it was now illegal. In 1654 we know that 300 of them armed themselves to prevent the king's troops destroying their crop. In 1667 Samuel Pepys recorded in his diary that lifeguards had been sent to Winchcombe 'to spoil the tobacco which people do plant there contrary to law'. The last reference I have found comes from 1691 when Richard Teale, a miller of Cheltenham, demanded recompense because the king's officers had destroyed his crop, despite being planted 'in ignorance of the law'.

Close encounters with Cheltenham Races

Three of my articles I wrote to coincide with Cheltenham's Gold Cup meeting in March each featured a local person. Here I have gathered the three articles together.

The Reverend Francis Close was a vocal opponent of the races amongst other aspects of the life of the spa town. His pre-race sermon at St Mary's (now Cheltenham Minster) in June 1827 sold 4,500 printed copies within a month. It still makes interesting reading.

Francis Close

FRANCIS CLOSE ARRIVED in Cheltenham as a young enthusiastic Anglican priest to be the curate of Holy Trinity (now just Trinity) church in Portland Street in 1824. Two years later he was appointed perpetual curate of St Mary's parish church; a post he held for the next thirty years. In the 1820s Cheltenham was not only attracting visitors to its waters but its permanent population was growing rapidly. Close entered this fast-moving world with the clear intention of raising the town's moral tone. So he campaigned tirelessly, for more schools and churches for the poor and for the cause of teetotalism, but also vigorously against the Roman Catholic religion and Irish immigration, the theatre, Sunday trains and the races. The pulpit in St Mary's church provided his main platform as people packed in to hear his lively, hard-hitting sermons.

On Sunday morning 17th June 1827, nicely timed ten days before the annual race meeting on Cleeve Common, he waded into "the evil consequences of attending the racecourse". Racegoers were "generally speaking, the least desirable visitors", who deterred the more numerous, more respectable visitors to the detriment of not only religion and morality, but also of trade. His image of the racegoers travelling up Cleeve Hill was at odds with the poem quoted in my earlier article on the races. He thundered, "And this I know, that the roads, and fields, and pathways, leading to the emporium of vice and folly, are strewn with the victims of vice

St Mary's church at the time of the controversy

and vicious excess." He also declared that down in the town, prostitution, licentiousness, drunkenness and violence were openly found on the streets. But worst of all was gambling, with its devastating effects on the town's lower orders. To ignore these problems was not good enough.

CHELTENHAM RACES,

TUESDAY, June 26, 1827.

THE St. LEGER STAKES of 25 Sovereigns each: for three-year-old colts, 8st. 7lb.; and fillies, 8st. 4lb.   Three Y. C. a mile.

A newspaper advert for the 1827 race meeting

Close challenged his congregation to go out and stop the races. The next year the grandstand at the race course was burnt down. Nobody was charged but rumours circulated that followers of Francis Close were responsible, although he himself would never have gone so far, as the guardian of Cheltenham's morals, to support the criminal act.

The sermon caused uproar around the town and a backlash appeared almost immediately. The editor of the *Gloucester and Cheltenham Herald* condemned Close for gross exaggeration. Another critic, Geoffrey Wildgoose, obviously a pseudonym, argued that the problem of drink was a thousand times more serious and that any mass meeting of people could give rise to abuses and evil. So should Close's packed church services therefore be banned? Behind another pseudonym Vindex condemned the vicar, 'Let the magistrates, and not the clergy, sort out vice.' he wrote.

No doubt such arguments provided interesting and even amusing reading for the literary classes of the town, both residents and visitors. For us they provide a fascinating insight into the concerns of Cheltenham nearly two hundred years ago, but in reality the controversy had little effect upon the races themselves. It was only as spas fell out of fashion that the races on Cleeve Hill finally faded away in 1842. Francis Close moved to become Dean of Carlisle in 1856; his name still commemorated by Dean Close School.

George Stevens was a jockey whose fame has been overshadowed by Fred Archer from Prestbury, who won 2,748 races and 13 Champion Jockey titles before killing himself aged twenty nine.

George Stevens (T.Curr)

G EORGE STEVENS WAS born in Cheltenham in 1833, the son of one of the countless servants to the leisured classes who lived in the town. He was still a teenager when his potential to be a successful jockey was recognised by William Holman, one of Cheltenham's famous trainers, who had his stables at Cleeve Lodge on Cleeve Common. There George was trained as a jockey so successfully that he won his first major race, the Wolverhampton Grand Annual, at the age of only eighteen. Then, just five years later, he came to wider attention by winning the Grand National at Aintree, riding *Free Trader*. This was the first of his five victories in the Grand National, a record which still stands today and which should have given the servant's son from Cheltenham the status of a superstar. The fact that he has never enjoyed the same fame as Fred Archer has much to do with the nature of horse racing at that time.

Fred Archer was a successful flat race jockey, riding thoroughbreds; George Stevens won over the jumps. When the Grand National was first run in 1839 it was designed for heavy hunters and cavalry horses and so clearly lacked the prestige of flat racing. However, at the time when George started on his career, the nature of steeple chasing was changing; fences were being lowered and the emphasis was moving to riding ex-flat race horses. In 1863 the start of the National was put back over a quarter of a mile to give more of a chase. Therefore it was little surprise that George's next two Grand National victories

Emblem Cottage in Stockwell Lane was named after the 1863 Grand National winner

were on the back of ex-flat racers: *Emblem* in 1863 and then *Emblematic* in 1864, which was described in the press as 'a rat' and 'too light and narrow-gutted'. The reward from the horses' owner, Lord Coventry of Earl's Croome, was enough for George to set himself up with his own small stable at the top of Stockwell Lane on Cleeve Hill.

Yet not long after this last victory, George left Lord Coventry, the earl considering the jockey had lost his nerve, and so George moved to his wife's uncle's

This stone on Old Road in Southam marks George Stevens fatal fall

training stables at Richard's Castle near Ludlow. It was here he trained *The Colonel*, 'of good girth with powerful shoulders and quarters', to such an effect that he rode him to victory in the Grand National in both 1869 and 1870, although only by a neck in the latter year. In 1871 he could only manage fourth place and the horse was retired to stud in Germany. George's last victory came shortly after this when he won at Cheltenham's Grand Annual meeting in April, riding his own mare, *Miss Dodson*.

And that's nearly the end of the story. Seven weeks later, on 1st June 1871, George had reached the Rising Sun Hotel on

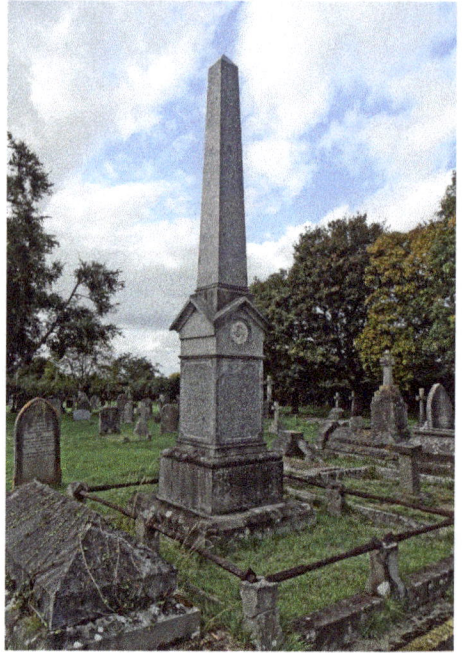

George's memorial in Cheltenham's cemetery was paid for by subscription

his way home from Cheltenham, when his cob, *The Clown*, for some reason bolted back down the hill, throwing George off in Southam where he cracked his head on the ground and never regained consciousness. It was a sadly ironical ending for a jockey who had ridden in fifteen Grand Nationals and won five of them with never a fall.

Adam Lindsay Gordon was a local lad, who became Australia's national poet

Adam Lindsay Gordon

I N 1847 A fourteen-year-old boy watched in excitement as horses and riders in Cheltenham's Grand Annual steeplechase flew past him through the fields on the lower slopes of Cleeve Hill around Prestbury. That boy was Adam Lindsay Gordon who became Australia's national poet. One of his most popular poems 'How We Beat the Favourite' describes an imaginary race which seems to have been based on that early experience on the edge of Cheltenham in 1847. What is the story behind the poem?

Although 'How We Beat the Favourite' only appeared in Australia in 1870, it contains enough clues for us to relate it to the steeplechasing around Cheltenham. A clue lies in the first line:

> 'Aye squire', said Stevens, 'they back him at evens;
> The race is all over, bar shouting, they say;
> The Clown ought to beat her; Dick Neville is sweeter
> Than ever - he swears he can win all the way.'

In all likelihood the reference was to George Stevens. Was it also coincidence that the poet's main rival *The Clown* was the name of Stevens' hacking horse, from which he fell to his death in Southam the year after the poem appeared? Adam Lindsay Gordon clearly intended his race to be set in England, referring to racing at Warwick and Aintree with *Abdelkadir*, the first horse to have won the Aintree Grand National in consecutive years, 1850-51, named as a competitor in the chase.

The poem gallops along at the breakneck speed of an actual race. As it progresses, most of the competitors fall by the wayside:

> The fourth fence, a wattle, floor'd Monk and Blue-bottle,
> The Drag came to grief at the blackthorn and ditch,
> The rails toppled over Redoubt and Red Rover,
> The lane stopped Lycurgus and Leicestershire Witch.
> She passed like an arrow Kildare and Cock Sparrow,
> And Mantrap and Mermaid refused the stone wall;
> And Giles on the Greyling came down at the paling,
> And I was left sailing, in front of them all.

Finally his mount *Iseult* is left to race neck and neck with *The Clown*. At the post it appears a dead heat but poetic licence creates a favourable conclusion;

> A nose I could swear by, but Clark said, 'The mare by
> A short head.' And that's how the favourite was beat.

As many poets before and after him, Adam was a troubled soul. Born in Charlton Kings he became a restless school boy with two short spells in Cheltenham College. Aged nineteen he stole a horse so he could compete in the Berkeley Hunt Cup. Was this the main reason his father offered to finance his emigration to Australia in August 1853 at the

As a schoolboy Adam Lindsay Gordon lived for a short time in this house with the plaque by the blue door, 28 Priory Street in Cheltenham

age of twenty? On the day of his departure he offered to give up this promise of a new life when he proposed to an unsuspecting seventeen year old, Jane Bridges. Not surprisingly she refused. Arriving in Australia he failed as a mounted policeman, a horse breaker and even a Member of Parliament in South Australia. It was steeplechasing and poetry that brought him fame. But steeplechasing was dangerous and in 1868 and 1870 he suffered head injuries from heavy falls. These seem to have aggravated his tendency to bouts of depression and the final straw came when he felt he had no money to pay his publisher for the book of poems which included 'How We Beat the Favourite'. The day after it was published, on 24th June 1870 he walked out of his house and shot himself. Sadly it was only later that he came to be honoured as Australia's national poet.

The statue of Adam Lindsay Gordon in Melbourne was erected in 1932

Private Harold Ashworth
16th Manchester Regiment

1st July 1916 remains the worst day in the history of the British army. By the end of the first day of the Battle of the Somme, some 20,000 troops had been killed and 40,000 wounded. In a departure from my usual article of local interest, to commemorate that centenary I chose to share my maternal grandfather's experience of the battle and its aftermath with readers of the magazine. Unlike many of the surviving soldiers, he recounted his experiences as a prisoner of war to my grandmother who then passed his story on to me. Little seems to have been written about prisoners in the First World War compared to the Second World War.

HAROLD WAS BORN in 1890 and had trained as a painter and decorator. He did not enlist until after his ailing mother died on 11th August 1915. Despite living in Oldham he joined the 16th Manchesters, which had been set up as a regiment specifically 'for clerks and warehousemen'. I don't know why he joined this regiment or how he trained, but his medals do not include the Star, indicating he had not gone abroad by the end of 1915, although the 16th Manchesters had first arrived in France on 6th November. We still have a copy of St John's gospel presented to him by his church dated 3rd April 1916, which perhaps indicates when he sailed to France.

The next glimpse of him comes in Trones Wood in northern France. The war diary of his regiment records that on 10th July 1916:

> 5am SA Coy report WOOD clear of Germans - four MGs sent up to assist in defence of WOOD
> 5:30am Germans re-occupied S portion of WOOD, presently cutting off some of our patrols who are still missing.

A family heirloom; a postcard from Harold as a prisoner of war to my grandmother, his future wife

Harold was a member of one of those patrols. He always blamed his inexperienced platoon commanding officer straight out of public school for his misfortune. Then, in one of those coincidences of war which probably only survived in the memory, he also claimed that he was not shot on capture because the German officer recognised Harold's company as the one which had allowed his own command to return to safety after they had strayed into Allied territory in the earlier confused fighting of that morning.

Harold was first taken to Dülmen prisoner of war camp not far from the present Dutch border, but was soon moved to Sprottau prisoner of war camp in Silesia (now Szprotawa in Poland) where he spent the rest of the war. Conditions there seem to have been

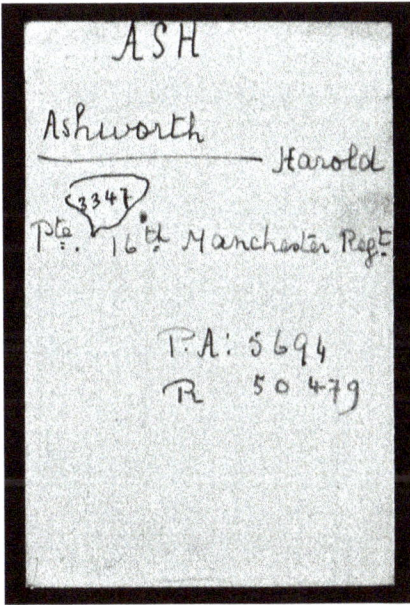

Harold's prisoner of war Red Cross record card

surprisingly favourable towards the prisoners, in contrast to what we might have expected after the experiences of many prisoners in the Second World War. They played football, were taken out to the local cinema, arranged dramas and musicals with printed programmes and even formed an orchestra. We know he was sent out to a farm at Bunzlau (now Boleslawiec) and I was delighted to have this confirmed when I found a photograph of him in a group of farmworkers in Albert Kendrick's online collection of images from Sprottau. As conditions for everyone in Germany were deteriorating, Harold always believed the farmer's wife saved him and his fellow prisoners of war from starving for she often dropped some of the bread she was taking to her chickens, despite this being a criminal offence. Even during the dark days

Accommodation huts at Sprottau PoW camp

One of the plays the prisoners created for the camp

of the blitz in Manchester during the Second World War, he would have nothing bad to say about the women of Germany.

Repatriation came in 1919 but he returned with one unwanted souvenir - a tapeworm from which he continued to suffer its debilitating effects for years. He resumed his pre-war trade and two years later married my grandmother. During the Second World War he took over his niece's newsagents in Manchester after her husband had been called up and he continued to run it until shortly before he died in 1954, leaving my grandmother a widow for thirty eight years. His wartime experiences probably contributed to his early death. Sixty two years later and exactly a century to the day, but not the time, his three grandchildren, myself, my sister Janet and cousin Kathryn, together with Margaret and

Englishmen working on farms in vicinity of Bunglau 1917

Harold is on the far right in the second row

Kathryn's husband Mike, made our own pilgrimage to Trones Wood to mark the occasion.

Our visit to Trones Wood 10th July 2016. Mike, Kathryn, Margaret, Janet and the author

Harold was one of the lucky ones who came back. A hundred years after the first day of the Battle of the Somme, I asked readers to please spare a thought for those who didn't.

Index

www.ingramcontent.com/pod-product-compliance
Lightning Source LLC
Chambersburg PA
CBHW051211090426
42740CB00022B/3462